The
Go
Grrrls
Workbook

The
Go
Grrrls
Workbook

Craig Winston LeCroy
and Janice Daley

W. W. Norton & Company
New York • London

For information about permission to reproduce selections from this book, write to Permissions, W. W. Norton & Company, Inc., 500 Fifth Avenue, New York, NY 10110

Manufacturing by Haddon Craftsmen
Book design and composition by Paradigm Graphics
Production Manager: Leeann Graham
Cover Illustration: Joanne Lew

ISBN 0-393-70348-7 (pbk.)

W. W. Norton & Company, Inc., 500 Fifth Avenue, New York, N.Y. 10110
www.wwnorton.com
W. W. Norton & Company, Ltd., Castle House, 75/76 Wells St., London W1T 3QT

2 3 4 5 6 7 8 9 0

This Go Grrrls Workbook belongs to

_____

I started this workbook on

_____

(Today's Date)

My birthday is

_____

Contents

The
Go
Grrrls
Workbook

Welcome to Go Grrrls!

What is Go Grrrls?

Go Grrrls is a fun club where all kinds of teenage girls can express themselves, learn new skills, and have fun.

Do I need to be a Go Grrrls club member to use this workbook?

No! If you are in a Go Grrrls club, your group leaders will ask you to do sections of the workbook as you go along. But even if you are not in the club, or if there isn't a Go Grrrls club near you, you can still do all of the activities in this book on your own. It might be more fun if you ask an adult that you really trust to read your work. Another way to enjoy the workbook, whether you are in the Go Grrrls club or not, is to share your work with your friends. Remember, whether you are in the "official" club or not, *you go, grrrl!*

What is in this workbook?

We're so glad you asked! This book has news you can use, fun quizzes to take, and all kinds of other activities for you to do. Here is a list of some of the features you will find in most chapters:

- **Slumber Party.** In every chapter, four friends have a slumber party. **Amanda, Caitlin, Sonya,** and **Trinecia** share their views, their secrets, their problems, and sometimes they just get silly.
- **Quiz Time.** These aren't the kinds of quizzes you take in school. Quiz Time is a fun way for you to think about yourself and answer questions to help you understand your actions and thoughts.
- **Did You Know?** offers interesting and important facts for you to learn.
- **Make It Happen.** This page suggests some actions that you might be able to take to make a change for the better.

- **Check It Out!** On these pages you put a check beside statements, words, or answers that are true just for you, or write your thoughts and feelings about issues that are important to teen girls.
- **Dear Suzie.** Suzie answers girls' questions with some good advice.
- **Paste-Up Page.** On these pages, you get to express your opinions (and your artistic talents) by drawing, writing, and making collages that show how you feel about important issues in your life.
- **Journal Assignments.** If you are attending a Go Grrrls club, your group leaders will ask you to fill out these pages before you come to each meeting. If you are not attending a Go Grrrls club, you can write your answers to the assignments and ask a trusted adult to go over them with you.

The best thing for you to remember as you go through this book is that you are an important part of the Go Grrrl community whether you are attending the club or not. Oh, and one more thing—remember to have fun! Ready to start? Well then, Go Grrrl!

Chapter 1
İntroduction to Go Grrrls

The First Slumber Party

Trinecia, Sonya, Caitlin, and Amanda are four friends who met at middle school. They are getting to know each other better, so they decided to have a slumber party. They like to share stories about their lives, their problems, their successes, and the people they care about.

Trinecia: I'm really glad you could all sleep over tonight. This is my first slumber party at my family's new house.

Sonya: Thanks for having us over, Trinecia. Your new house is cool.

Amanda: Yeah, I like your bedroom. I have to share a room with my two little sisters and they're such a pain.

Trinecia: I used to share my room, too, but my older sister just left for college so now I've got my own space. Now I can put up my posters without fighting about what should be on the walls. Mostly it's great, but I actually kind of miss her.

Caitlin: I know what you mean. I have an older sister, too, and I always thought she bugged me until she moved out. Then I wished she was around to bug me some more.

Trinecia: I hear that. There are some things that are just easier to talk to your sister about than anybody else. I sure can't talk to my little brother about anything. All he cares about is his stupid video games. And my mom is pretty cool about stuff, but . . . you know, she's my mother!

Amanda: But you can talk to us now, Trinecia! Ever since we started middle school you guys have been my best friends. Let's swear that we'll talk to each other about our most important stuff.

Sonya: I'm up for that. Maybe we could take turns having slumber parties at each others' houses. . . . I don't know why, but sometimes it's just easier to talk about really personal things when it's late at night.

Caitlin: Or really early in the morning, like it is right now! I love talking at 2:00 A.M.!

Trinecia: You go, girl! I'll swear if you all will.

Amanda: Okay, we're all in, then. We could call ourselves the "Go Grrrls"!

Sonya: I think you need some sleep, Amanda.

Caitlin: I kind of like that name.

Trinecia: Yeah, me too.

Sonya: All right.

Sonya does a forward somersault on the floor and then jumps up and shouts, "Go Grrrls rule!" Everybody laughs.

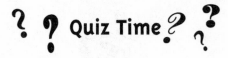

The Go Grrrls Puzzle

Here is a puzzle that shows you all of the different things we will be talking about in this book and in the Go Grrrls club. Every piece of the puzzle is important.

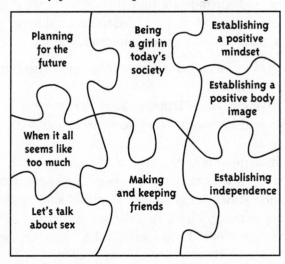

Your ideas and thoughts are important, too. Circle all of the topics in the list below that you think are important in your life. We'll talk about all of these in this Go Grrrls workbook.

☞ *Planning for the Future*

☞ **Being a Girl in Today's Society**

☞ **Establishing a Positive Body Image**

☞ LET'S TALK ABOUT SEX

☞ *Establishing a Positive Mindset*

☞ **Establishing Independence**

☞ **Making and Keeping Friends**

☞ WHEN IT ALL SEEMS LIKE TOO MUCH

☞ *Media Messages*

Did You Know?

Girls' Bill of Rights*

Girls have a right to be themselves—people first and females second—and to resist pressure to behave in sex-stereotyped ways.

- **Girls have a right** to express themselves with originality and enthusiasm.
- **Girls have a right** to take risks, to strive freely, and to take pride in success.
- **Girls have a right** to accept and enjoy the bodies they were born with and not to feel pressured to compromise their health in order to satisfy the dictates of an "ideal" physical image.
- **Girls have a right** to be free of vulnerability and self-doubt and to develop as mentally and emotionally sound individuals.
- **Girls have a right** to prepare for interesting work and economic independence.

 Check It Out!

Describing Ourselves

Let's start with something really upbeat. It is important to notice the positive qualities that we have. The list on this page has lots of positive adjectives that can describe a person. Put a check mark next to the ones that you think describe you. Then look at the words that have the same letter (or sound) as your first name. Choose one of these as your own personal description. For example, if your name is Lavinia, you could call yourself "Luminous Lavinia." Feel free to add any adjectives that aren't on the list, too!

Able	Assertive	Candid	Compassionate	Dependable
Accomplished	Astute	Capable	Confident	Determined
Active	Balanced	Carefree	Cool	Dignified
Adaptable	Beautiful	Caring	Courageous	Diligent
Adept	Beneficent	Centered	Creative	Direct
Admirable	Benevolent	Cerebral	Curious	Disciplined
Adorable	Blissful	Charismatic	Daring	Distinctive
Adventuresome	Bold	Cheerful	Dashing	Divine
Affectionate	Brave	Classy	Dazzling	Dynamic
Amazing	Bright	Clever	Decisive	Eager
Artistic	Brilliant	Colorful	Dedicated	Easygoing

*Girls Incorporated Bill of Rights reprinted with permission from Girls Incorporated ® 2000.

Eclectic
Ecstatic
Effective
Electrifying
Elegant
Enchanting
Encouraging
Energetic
Enlightened
Enthusiastic
Excellent
Exciting
Expressive
Extraordinary
Exuberant
Fabulous
Famous
Fantastic
Fascinating
Feisty
Flexible
Focused
Foresighted
Forthright
Frank
Freethinking
Friendly
Fun
Gallant
Generous
Genial
Gentle
Genuine
Gifted
Glamorous
Glowing

Gorgeous
Graceful
Great
Grounded
Gutsy
Happy
Hardy
Harmonious
Healthy
Helpful
Heroic
Honest
Honorable
Hopeful
Humane
Idealistic
Imaginative
Imperial
Important
Impressive
Independent
Individualistic
Ingenious
Insightful
Intelligent
Interesting
Intrepid
Inventive
Jolly
Jovial
Joyful
Jubilant
Judicious
Just
Kind
Knowledgeable

Laid-back
Learned
Levelheaded
Lionhearted
Lively
Logical
Lovable
Loyal
Luminous
Magical
Magnetic
Magnificent
Majestic
Marvelous
Masterful
Memorable
Merry
Mighty
Mindful
Motivated
Natural
Nervy
Nice
Noble
Nonjudgmental
Noteworthy
Observant
Open-minded
Optimistic
Organized
Original
Outgoing
Outstanding
Passionate
Patient
Perceptive

Persistent
Perspicacious
Persuasive
Pioneering
Playful
Poetic
Positive
Powerful
Principled
Profound
Proud
Quick-witted
Radiant
Rational
Reflective
Regal
Reliable
Remarkable
Resilient
Resolute
Resourceful
Rhythmic
Righteous
Robust
Sassy
Satisfied
Scholarly
Scrupulous
Secure
Sensible
Serene
Shining
Skillful
Smart
Smooth
Solid

Spirited
Sprightly
Steady
Strong
Stunning
Successful
Superb
Sweet
Talented
Tenacious
Tender
Terrific
Thoughtful
Thrilling
Tolerant
Tough
Triumphant
Unique
Unstoppable
Upstanding
Valorous
Vibrant
Victorious
Virtuous
Vivacious
Warm
Well-read
Wholehearted
Wholesome
Wise
Witty
Wonderful
Youthful
Zealous
Zestful

Dear Suzie

Dear Suzie,

I just started middle school this year and I am having kind of a hard time. In my grade school I knew all the kids and the teachers, too. I'm excited about being in middle school, but sometimes I get really nervous cause I don't know anybody in my classes and we change from one teacher to another every hour. I run from one class to the next and look down at my feet so I don't have to worry about who to say hello to, or about how many kids I don't know at all. It just feels like nobody knows me here! It makes me feel really self-conscious about what I say and what I look like. Do you have any suggestions for me?

Nervous in New Jersey

Dear Nervous,

You are very good at describing your new experience. New experiences can definitely make us nervous, but we can help ourselves relax in several ways. It sounds like one thing that is making you feel anxious is that you don't have classes with the same friends that you did last year. Connecting with friends is important, but it takes some time to do that. May you could check out some clubs at your school. All kinds of things might be available: You might be able to join Go Grrrls, chess, drama, soccer, or a foreign language club. Maybe you're interested in student government or working on the school yearbook. Once you think about what you're interested in, you can hook up with other people who share your interests.

Transitions (changes that we make) can challenge us to discover new things about ourselves. So hook up with some friends, think about your interests, and remind yourself that it's perfectly natural to feel a bit nervous. If you need to talk more about it you can find a counselor at your school who can give you some good suggestions.

Good luck,
Suzie

Paste-Up Page

Brilliant Buddies

Write down your adjective and name, and the adjectives and names of other people in your Go Grrrls club or other friends of yours at school and in your neighborhood. If they cannot think of an adjective to describe themselves, show them the list and help them pick out something positive! You might want to have your "brilliant buddies" autograph this page themselves. You could have them sign in all different colors or draw a little symbol by their names. Have fun!

Your First Journal Assignment

All about Me

Fill in the blanks below with personal information that is all about you. You can share your list with your friends.

My *favorite* color is _____

My *favorite* song is _____

My *favorite* music group is _____

My *favorite* book is _____

My *favorite* TV show is _____

I have _____ pets. I have _____
  (How many?)   (What kind of pets are they?)

Their names are: _____

At home, I live with (put a check mark next to everyone who lives at home with you):

Mother	Father	Sister (How many?)	Brother (How many?)
Stepmother	Stepfather	Step or half sisters (How many?)	Step or half brothers (How many?)
Guardian	Aunt	Uncle	Cousins
Foster mother	Foster father	Group home (How many kids live there?)	Other (Who else?)

My hobbies are:

Reading	Writing poems & stories	Dancing	Singing
Surfing the net	Playing soccer	Rollerblading	Riding my bicycle
Skiing	Playing tennis	Learning about different cultures	Ballet
Playing a musical instrument	Drawing/Painting	Other sports What are they?	Write in your own:

Chapter 2
Being a Girl in Today's Society

Media Messages

Do you watch TV? Read magazines? Listen to music? Surf the Internet? Go to the movies? Television, magazines, music, the Internet, and movies are all different kinds of media. And when you watch, read, listen, and surf you will definitely start to discover some "media messages." In this section, you will learn to think about what these media messages are and what the media is telling you about what it means to be a girl in today's society.

Slumber Party

Caitlin: Happy Friday night everybody!

Sonya: Yeah, happy Friday! I had a pretty great week. Sean said hi to me three times in the hall today, I figured out how to play a new guitar chord, and I totally aced my third-period social studies test.

Amanda: Way to be, Sonya! That was Ms. Arthur's test wasn't it? I have her, too, in 5th period.

Sonya: Yep. She's really cool. She always talks about stuff that I care about in her class. Like she talks about the environment, and things that affect teenagers.

Amanda: I did really well on that test, too.

Trinecia: What was your test on, you guys?

Sonya: We studied some ways that media—TV, music, magazines, and stuff like that—can influence our opinions.

Amanda: Yeah, and one thing we learned about are stereotypes—you know, stereotypes are when people describe everybody from a group as if they acted the same way. And usually the descriptions are nasty. So we were talking about stereotypes, and then we learned that the media spreads some nasty stereotypes about women.

Caitlin: I talked about this with my mom once. She and I sat down together and watched TV for a whole night. A bunch of the women we saw were, like, totally skinny, and they were all acting like they forgot they had a brain. It was depressing!

Trinecia: I know what you mean. I bought a magazine last week because—well, actually because I wanted to read my horoscope in it—but then when I looked through the rest of it, I started getting pissed off about all the ads. There were more ads than articles! And the models in the ads were mostly skinny white girls with totally perfect teeth and skin.

Amanda: So are we all supposed to spend our whole entire lives thinking about what we look like?

Sonya: That's definitely one of the media messages but that's not the only one. We're all supposed to have sex all the time, too.

Everybody screams and laughs.

Trinecia: Sonya!

Sonya: Well that *is* another message. Caitlin, can we turn on your TV for a second?

Caitlin: Sure, go ahead.

They turn on a TV station with music videos.

Amanda: I love this song.

Sonya: I do, too, Amanda. But look at the girls in this video. They all look like they just want to jump this guy's bones.

Trinecia: You are a wild woman, Sonya!

Sonya: No, no, no. But look. Would you wear those red vinyl shorts to school?

Everybody screams and laughs again.

Amanda: No way! But I still like the song.

Caitlin: When my mom and I talked about this, she said that it's cool to still listen to the music and watch videos . . . but that you have to think about what you see and hear. She and I sometimes "shout back" at the tube when it shows a woman doing something really stupid.

Sonya: Ms. Arthur had us do a fun assignment, too. She gave us a bunch of magazines and had us rip out some ads. Then we changed the words and the pictures in the ad to make fun of the way they were trying to influence us.

Trinecia: What do you mean?

Amanda: Well, I cut out an ad for beer that had some dumpy guy with these three tall, beautiful girls hanging all over him. They were all drinking beer and smiling. Then I changed it so that the guy was throwing up from drinking too much, and the models were all holding their noses!

Caitlin: That's disgusting. Thank you for sharing!

Amanda: Yeah, but you know they always try to make those ads so glamorous. In real life, drinking isn't always like that.

Sonya: I know. Let's go through some magazines now and change some "ads" into "bads," if you know what I mean.

Caitlin: Great idea. And I'll go make some popcorn so we can eat some . . . and throw some at the TV screen when these videos show women doing stupid stuff!

Trinecia: Yeah! Party, party, party!

They all laugh.

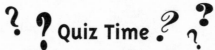

Read each sentence then choose your best answer by circling the letter next to it. Have fun!

1. Each week, I spend _____ hours watching TV.

A. 0–2 hours
B. 2–5 hours
C. 5–10 hours
D. 10–15 hours
E. More than 15 hours per week

2. I think that *most* television shows and commercials show women as:

A. Smart and in charge
B. Clueless and ditzy
C. Most important for their ideas
D. Most important for their appearance
E. Both B and D

3. Most of the articles and ads I see in teen magazines are about:

A. How to develop my creativity (writing, drawing, music, etc.)
B. Physical appearance (clothes, make-up, exercise, dieting, etc.)
C. Scientific discoveries
D. Boys, boys, boys
E. Both B and D

4. When I watch music videos on television, I usually find that:

A. The girls are wearing much more clothing than the guys are
B. The girls in the videos look just like most women I know
C. The music lyrics talk a lot about how smart and kind women are
D. The girls are usually wearing skimpy clothes

Answers

1. How many hours do you spend watching TV?

Well, of course, you are the only one who knows how many hours you spend watching the tube, so we can't tell you what the "right" answer is. We can tell you some other things, though.

If your answer was . . .

D or E:

If you watch at least 10 hours of TV each week, guess what? Chances are pretty good that you are being influenced by some of the messages that are in the programs you watch. You will get a lot of information in this chapter about how to think critically about those messages. For example, what do most of the women look like on the shows you see? Are they very thin models? What about the guys? Are they very thin models, too? Hmmm. How about the way women television characters act? Are they calm, intelligent, and confident or are they nervous and clueless? Let's keep thinking about this. And just as an experiment, you might want to try to watch less than 10 hours of TV this week. Try to notice the different fun things you do instead.

C:

If you watch 5–10 hours of TV each week, you are doing a great job of escaping the mind-numbing tube! Still, even that much TV is enough for you to get some negative messages about women. It's smart to keep your eyes open for stupid commercials and shows that send negative messages about women.

A or B:

If you watch 0–2 hours of TV each week, congratulations! You must be very busy with other things or else you just aren't into the TV thing. The less TV you watch, the less likely you are to think the television characters are like real life!

2. I think most television shows and commercials show women as . . .

Your answer might depend on how much you've thought about the TV shows you watch or on what kind of shows you usually watch. For example, if your answer was . . .

A or C:

If you answered that television programs show women as smart, in charge, and important for their ideas, then you are probably watching some science, nature, history, or public television shows. Keep at it. It's great that there really *are* some programs we can turn to that show women as the smart and accomplished people they are, right? Right! But keep an eye out for those negative messages, too. They're out there.

B, D, or E:

If you answered that most television shows and commercials show women as clueless, ditzy, and most important for their appearance, then you are probably already starting to think crit-

ically about the media messages you're getting. Good job! The first step in being able to
escape from negative media messages is being able to recognize what they are.

3. Most of the articles in teen magazines are about . . .
Your answer might depend on how much you've thought about the magazines you read or on
what *kind* of magazines you usually read, just like the last question. For example, if your
answer was . . .

A or C:
If you answered that most teen magazines are about things like creativity and scientific discoveries, then you're probably already reading some great girls' zines (magazines written for
and by girls). There are some wonderful magazines available that are written by, for, and
about great girls like you. Keep reading those!

B, D, or E:
If you answered that most teen magazines are about appearance and boys then you are already
starting to identify some of the messages in magazines. Is appearance the most important
thing in the whole world? Of course not. Does wearing the perfect shade of mascara make
somebody a fantastic person? No! Should girls be walking around 24/7 thinking about boys
only? Well, no, thanks—girls have a *life!*

4. When I watch music videos I usually find that . . .
Okay, your answer to this one might depend on what you've been watching lately, but if you're
watching any music videos at all, chances are good that you've seen some really negative
images of women. If your answer was:

A:
Wow! If the girls are wearing more than the guys in the videos you're watching, share that
station with your friends! Seriously, so many videos tend to show women in skimpy clothing
that it's hard to imagine one that doesn't.

B:
Again, wow! If the girls in the videos look just like most women you know, share the station
with your friends! You know what we mean, right? So many videos show really, really thin
women dressed in high heels and tiny little outfits. Their skin is perfect, their teeth are white
and straight, and they never have a "bad hair day." Is this real? Hmmm—nope!

C:
Triple wow! If the lyrics of your favorite music videos talk a lot about how smart and kind
women are, congratulations on your excellent taste! There are some great songs out there that
do celebrate women's strength, tenderness, and brilliance. But too many others put women
down.

D:

No surprises here if you picked this answer. Yep, a lot of girls on the music videos are wearing skimpy clothes. What's up with this anyway? Do girls walk around in bikinis on the street all the time? Why are the guys all fully dressed? Could there be a negative message suggesting that men should have more power than women? There could be, but we don't like the message. Let's talk some more about this subject!

Did You Know?

Girls and the Media

Many teen magazines designed for girls contain more ads than articles.

Many teens are exposed to 400 to 600 ads every day. (Through a combination of television, radio, magazines, newspapers, and the Internet).

The Journal of the American Medical Association states that the average teenager listens to 10,500 hours of rock music between the 7th and 12th grades. (What are the messages in the music?)

In real life, super models don't really look like they do on television or in the magazines. There are special techniques used to improve their images. Computerized photo editing can erase blemishes, make people appear thinner than they are, change a profile, etc. No wonder they look so darned perfect!

Some companies that make alcohol and tobacco try to get girls to use their products by making the people in their advertisements look really glamorous. (Are we gonna fall for that?! I don't think so!)

 # Check It Out

Talking Back to Media Messages

Trinecia, Amanda, Caitlin, and Sonya had some great ideas for "talking back" to media messages. On this page, circle or check off any of the activities that you could do to talk back to media messages that you run into.

☐ Write a letter to the editor of your favorite magazine. Tell them about some of the stereotypes about women that you see in their magazine articles and advertising.

☐ Watch TV with your family or friends and take some notes about how you think women are being portrayed in TV shows and commercials.

☐ Listen carefully to the lyrics of some of your favorite music. Do any of the lyrics put down women? If so, rewrite some lyrics of your own to change the song!

☐ Go to an Internet chat room and start a conversation with other kids about the media messages you notice. (Remember to "surf safely." Don't give your name and information to strangers!)

☐ Surf the Internet or go to a good local bookstore to find special magazines (sometimes called "zines") that challenge the stereotypes about girls.

☐ Cut out a magazine or newspaper ad that shows alcohol or tobacco as glamorous. Change the ad so that it shows some real-life hazards of using those substances.

☐ Ask your social studies teacher if your class can do a unit on media messages.

Write in your own idea here:

I AM UNIQUE!

One great way to stop worrying about what the media says we ought to be like is to explore your creativity. To help you discover what is unique and special about you, fill in the blanks of the poem below. Read your poem out loud. Share it with your family. Remember that who you are inside—your hopes, dreams, talents, skills, and ideas—are important.

My name is _____.
                    (your name, backwards)

_____ dream of me at night and
(Plural favorite animal)

_____ sing my name at dawn.
(Plural favorite flower)

I am older than _____,
                    (an emotion: use the noun form of the word)

and as wise as (the) _____.
                    (natural force, object, or place you love)

My name is _____.
                    (your name, backwards, again)

Dear Suzie

Dear Suzie,

I am 13 years old and in the 8th grade. My whole life I've always been really into sports. I play soccer, basketball, and volleyball with my brothers and other kids who live on my street, and I'm usually one of the first kids picked when we choose teams. In other words, I'm really good! But I've been reading a lot of teen magazines lately, and none of them really talk about the stuff that I'm interested in. I am starting to feel kind of weird about being an athlete.

I've even noticed that some of my old friends who used to play sports have stopped playing and all they want to do is go to the shopping mall. I like clothes, but I just think it's boring to cruise around the mall all Saturday. My friend Laura is starting to call me a "jock-o tomboy," which I guess is okay, but she says it like there's something wrong with that. This is the first year I've even considered not going out for the hoops team, because I'm getting tired of getting called names. What do you think about this?

Tomboy in Tennessee

Dear Tomboy,

From your description I can tell that you are a talented athlete. What a wonderful gift to have the skills that you have! You are also right to notice that most of the magazines (and other media) that are designed for girls your age put way too much emphasis on fashion and makeup. They hardly ever talk about other important subjects like education, social issues, careers, and sports! Don't let the media messages (or friends who have been brainwashed by them!) stop you from using your natural gifts.

Did you know that girls who play sports:

- often have higher self-esteem than girls who don't play sports?
- have a more positive body image than girls who don't play sports?
- learn important skills about how to set goals, how to work as a team, and how to deal with failures, which are all really important experiences?
- are 50% less likely to smoke cigarettes?

So pursue your athletic goals and be proud. You might also want to subscribe to some of the newer magazines (or "zines") that are spreading the word that girls are about a lot more than just makeup and clothes! You could even write a fan letter to one of the new stars of the women's NBA to ask about life as a professional athlete. By the way, when your friends call you names like "tomboy," tell them you are proud to be talented. You Go Grrrl!

Suzie

Page

Stereotypes of Women

Time to raid some magazines! Look through magazines and newspapers that you have around the house. (Make sure it's okay to shred them.) On this page, glue in some pictures and words that portray women in stereotypical ways. On the next page, glue in pictures and words that portray women in nonstereotypical ways. When you finish, compare the words and images. What magazines and papers did you get most of the images from? You might want to share this paste-up page with your social studies teacher.

Page

Real Women: Not Stereotypes!

Journal Assignment

Five Things I Like about Myself

We have been talking about how important it is to think critically about media messages that stereotype women and girls. These messages can sometimes cause girls to feel badly about themselves. By thinking critically and "talking back" at these messages, girls can free themselves from the false idea that they have to act and look like the stereotypes.

In the next chapter we are going to talk about more ways for girls to feel good about themselves. For this journal assignment, your task is to make a list of five things you like about yourself. You can do it!

1.

2.

3.

4.

5.

Now share at least three of these items with your Go Grrrls pals!

Chapter 3
Establishing a Positive Body Image

Bodies are amazing. They come in so many different shapes, colors, and sizes. Just think about how your own body has changed since you were a little girl! So why do so many girls wish that their own bodies looked different? In this chapter we are going to talk about some of the reasons that many girls are dissatisfied with their bodies. We will also talk about ways to enjoy your body and appreciate it!

Slumber Party

Sonya: I'm so glad you could all come over to my house tonight. Let's dig into this pizza that my mom ordered for us.

Trinecia: Looks good to me. I'll take a vegetarian slice, please.

Amanda: Not me! Give me some of that pepperoni, okay?

Sonya: You got it. Which do you want, Caitlin?

Caitlin: Um. I don't really want any. I'm on a diet.

Trinecia: You're on a *what?*

Caitlin: You know, on a diet. I look like a beached whale and I'm sick of being fat.

Amanda: Caitlin, you are *so* not fat. Where did you get that idea?

Caitlin: I don't know. Well, actually, my mom called me "pudgy" last week. Pudgy! God I hate that word. I just about cried. And then in the hall on Thursday, Joey Norton snorted like a pig when I walked by. (She starts to cry.)

Sonya: That is so, so rude. It's all right, Caitlin. Joey has the IQ of a rock and the personality of a garbage can.

Trinecia: That's right. You're one of the healthiest people I know, Caitlin. Remember when you and I took that hike up the Violet Trail last month? You were cruising ahead of everybody.

Amanda: Yeah, and you're the one who taught us all that line dance. You can really move!

Caitlin: Thanks, you guys. I know I'm good at hiking and dancing, but no matter what I do I just don't get skinny.

Sonya: You know, not everybody's body is supposed to be super skinny. Remember how we just all shouted back at the TV for trying to tell everybody that women are supposed to look like sticks?

Amanda: Yeah, and we can't look like sticks. Ms. Hawkinson told us in health class that girls are supposed to weigh more when we get to middle school. She even called it . . . you won't believe this one . . . a "fat spurt"!

Trinecia: Now I have to say that sounds disgusting.

Amanda: I know, I know, but wait a minute. All it means is that when girls get to a certain age . . .

Caitlin: You're talking about puberty. That's another word I hate.

Amanda: All right, then, when we start to mature our bodies need to develop more fat to be healthy. If we didn't, then our bodies wouldn't be ready to get periods and stuff.

Trinecia: Like *that* would be a problem.

Sonya: I hear you, but you know it would be a drag to always stay a little girl and never turn into a full-fledged wild woman!

Caitlin: But you guys, there's nothing wrong with dieting.

Trinecia: You know, I read that it's healthier not to really diet, but to exercise and eat what you need. Just focus on eating when you're hungry and eating a lot of different kinds of food. Like one day you might have celery with peanut butter on it for a snack and another day you might have an apple with some peanut butter, and sometimes you might have some *pizza!*

She opens the pizza box and pulls out a big slice and takes a big bite.

Caitlin: What about my mom telling me I should be skinnier?

Sonya: I think you need to sit down and talk to your mom about that. Or maybe you could go to that nice counselor at school, Ms. Keating, and ask her about ways to talk to your mom.

Caitlin: Maybe I will.

Trinecia: Yeah, and I think all of us need to stick together. Let's swear that we will concentrate on being our best selves, whatever that is.

Amanda: Pinkie swear! Now pass that pizza over here.

?? Quiz Time ??

How do you feel about your own body? Take the quiz below to find out if you might be able to improve your body image.

1. When I am out with my friends, I constantly compare myself with them to see who weighs more:

A. Never
B. Hardly ever
C. Sometimes
D. Frequently
E. Always

2. When I think about how my body looks, I usually feel:

A. Proud of how I look
B. Pretty satisfied with how I look
C. Just okay about how I look
D. Pretty dissatisfied with how I look
E. Terrible about how I look

3. I would describe my body as:

A. Strong, healthy, and cool
B. A pretty good place to live in
C. Just all right, I guess
D. Kind of ugly
E. Don't even go there. I don't want to talk about it.

4. I think that appearance (the way a person looks) is the most important thing about girls.

A. Totally disagree
B. Disagree somewhat
C. Not sure
D. Agree somewhat
E. Completely agree

5. When I think about food:

A. It sounds good and I get hungry
B. I think of my favorite foods
C. I don't really think about it much
D. I feel guilty just thinking about food because I don't want to gain weight
E. I get really tense and nervous and feel terrible when I even think about eating

6. I think exercise:

A. Is a good way to stay healthy

B. Helps my mind and my body feel good

C. Is something I think about doing but really haven't gotten around to it

D. Is absolutely necessary so that I can keep losing weight

E. Is for fools. Give me a bag of chips and the TV, thanks

7. When I look at magazines or watch TV:

A. I am glad that I have my own unique style

B. I feel sorry for the boring people in charge of the media who seem to think that there is only one way to look attractive

C. I'm not sure how I feel about the images I see

D. I feel kind of bad about my body and looks

E. I always put myself down for not looking like the skinny models

8. When I feel upset about something:

A. I talk to a friend

B. I take a long walk to chill out

C. I'm not sure what I usually do

D. I go on a really strict diet just to show that I have some control in the world

E. I eat a whole bag of cookies and follow that up with a carton of chocolate ice cream

9. I think that healthy people:

A. Come in all shapes and sizes

B. Are lucky to have the gift of health

C. I don't really think about "health"

D. Must be skinny

E. Have the right to tease people who are out of shape

10. When I look at myself in the mirror:

A. I am proud that I resemble people who I care about in my family

B. I am happy that my body is strong and healthy

C. I guess I look just okay

D. I pick out certain characteristics that I'm really unhappy with (my thighs, my nose, etc.)

E. I put myself down for every characteristic that doesn't look "perfect" to me

Answers

If you answered mostly As and Bs:
Congratulations! You have a great attitude about your body! You feel good about being unique and you don't worry about what other people or the media say you "should" look like. You care about your health and take care of yourself without worrying too much about it. You can set a strong example for your friends by sharing your positive attitude with them. Your body confidence will help you to be confident in other areas of your life, too.

If you answered mostly Cs:
You probably haven't quite figured out how you feel about your body. You're not completely happy with the way you look, but you're not obsessed about your appearance, either. Now is a great time to start exploring ways to be healthy and feel good about the unique person that you are. You might start by thinking about all of the great qualities, inside and out, that you have. Celebrate the fact that there is nobody else on earth who can look, feel, and act exactly like you!

If you answered mostly Ds and Es:
You probably spend a lot of time worrying about how you look. You may spend a lot of time wishing you had the so-called perfect body . . . without realizing that your own body and unique style is something to celebrate! You are not alone. Many girls feel badly about their appearance at some time, but they *can* learn to appreciate themselves. You might need some help to start feeling good about the way you look. Start by talking to an adult you trust. You could show him or her this quiz as a way to start the conversation. And remember, you are somebody special, inside and out!

Did You Know?

Eating Disorders

People with eating disorders often use these self-destructive behaviors as a way of dealing with other life problems. Fifteen percent of young women in the United States have some kind of eating problem. Here are the facts:

Anorexia nervosa
- Anorexia is a disorder in which people are preoccupied with dieting and looking thin, which leads to too much weight loss. Often anorexics will not admit (to themselves or others) that they have a problem or that they are "afraid of fat."
- One percent of U.S. teen girls develop anorexia, and up to 10% of that 1% die from the disorder.

- About 1,000 people die of anorexia nervosa every year.
- Some danger signs of anorexia include:
    losing a lot of weight
    skipping or stopping monthly menstrual periods
    hair loss
    cold hands and feet
    compulsive exercise
    lying to others about food
    depression
    growth of fine body hair on arms, legs, and other areas
    heart tremors
    dry skin
    shortness of breath
- Anorexia can lead to bone mineral loss, low blood pressure, and irregular heartbeat (which can cause a heart attack).

Bulimia nervosa
- Bulimia is a disorder where people tend to eat a lot of food in one sitting (binge) and almost always throw up or use laxatives afterwards (purge). Usually the person realizes that this behavior is not normal or healthy.
- Up to 5% of U.S. college women are bulimic.
- Bulimics can have a variety of body weights . . . they are not always extremely thin like anorexics.
- Danger signs of bulimia include:
    vomiting, using laxatives or diuretics to try to lose weight
    depression
    swollen glands in the face and neck
    sore throat
    irregular menstrual periods
    dental problems
    vomiting blood
    weakness
- Bulimia can lead to long-term damage of the liver, kidney, and bowels.
- Bulimia can also cause irregular heartbeat, which can lead to a heart attack.

Binge eating
- People with binge eating disorder usually cannot control their eating and keep their binging secret.
- Binge eaters do not purge like bulimics do.
- Up to 40% of people who are obese could be binge eaters.

- Some danger signs of binge eating include:
    feeling like you cannot control eating
    eating when you're not hungry
    feelings of shame
    depression
    obesity

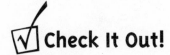 **Check It Out!**

Establishing a Positive Body Image

Check out all of the things you can do to get and keep a positive body image. Then circle or check off three things that you will try this week!

☐ Don't think of your body as "pieces and parts." (For example, don't pick out parts like your thighs or your butt that you don't like!) Think of yourself as one whole, cool package. You are!

☐ Go one whole day without looking in the mirror even once! What do you notice?

☐ Be nice to your body. Do things that feel good, like taking a glorious bath, or giving yourself a manicure.

☐ Move around! Just get up and dance to a song you like when you hear it on the radio. Play with your dog. Go for a walk with your pals. Being active can help your mind and your body feel good.

☐ Make a list of ten things you like about yourself that are *not* related to your body. (Hint: You can use the big list of adjectives from chapter one of this book to give you some ideas!)

☐ Declare a "no put-downs day" where you and your friends agree to say only nice things about yourselves. How do you feel after a whole day of this?

☐ Eat when you are hungry and eat until you are full, then stop.

☐ Count how many ads there are for diets and diet products in the magazines in your house. How many of these ads are aimed at women? How many are aimed at men? What's up with that?!

☐ When you see yourself in the mirror, think about how cool it is that the way you look is linked, through your genes, to your ancestors. Do you look like your great aunt Freda who owned her own ranch? Do your hands look just like your mom's hands? What a great connection to make!

What I Like about My Body

Complete the following statements. Think about all the different aspects of your body that you like.

Example: *What I like about my body is that I have beautiful hands with long fingers.*

what I like about my body is _____

_____

What i like about my body is _____

_____

What I like about my body is _____

_____

What i Like about MY body iʃ _____

_____

WHAT I LIKE ABOUT MY BODY IS _____

_____

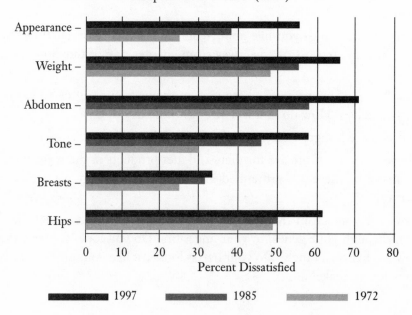

WOMEN'S DISSATISFACTION WITH THEIR BODIES.
Adapted from Garner (1997)

Percent Dissatisfied

■ 1997   ■ 1985   ■ 1972

Dear Suzie

Dear Suzie,

Most people think I am a really normal, happy person but I am keeping a secret that is starting to get scary. It's too gross to tell anybody about, so I thought I might be able to write about it instead. On the outside everything seems okay. I am a cheerleader, I get really good grades, I am pretty popular, and all that stuff. But I do this thing that I'm really embarrassed to tell anybody about. Sometimes when I'm at home by myself I eat a whole bunch of food and then I kind of make myself throw up afterwards. I usually feel really ashamed of myself right after I do it.

I don't do it all the time, but I think I've been doing it more lately. My cousin, Marilyn, taught me how when I slept over at her house one night. She said it helps her stay skinny. But I'm not even skinny. I'm afraid that if I stop doing this that I'll get really fat, but lately I'm even more scared about the way my body is feeling. My throat is sore a lot, and I feel really tired all the time. What can I do?

Scared in Cincinnati

Dear Scared,

I am very glad that you wrote to me. I think you already suspect that you are wrestling with an eating disorder. When people eat a lot of food (binge) and then throw up (purge) it is called "bulimia nervosa." The most important thing for you to know is that you need to get someone else to help you with this problem. It is a scary secret for you to keep, but you can get better once you tell somebody what's happening.

You are not alone. Many girls and women have some kind of eating disorder. Sadly, eating disorders ruin many girls' health. In some cases, eating disorders can cause very serious, long-term health problems or even death. This is not something for you to keep secret. It is important for you to know that you can get help. I thank you for trusting me enough to write to me. Please talk to an adult you trust, your school nurse, your school social worker or counselor, your doctor, or even a local telephone help line. You can also read more about eating disorders in the library or on the Internet. Remember that being skinny is not the same thing as being healthy. It's time to think of what will help your whole self—mind, body, and spirit—feel good. Write back to me soon.

Suzie

Journal Assignment

Five Negative Things I Sometimes Tell Myself

In this chapter we talked about how to establish a positive body image. In the next chapter we are going to keep talking about how to achieve a positive self image, but we are going to focus a lot more on the kind of things we say to ourselves with our inner voice. Your journal assignment is to write five negative things you sometimes say to yourself. Don't worry, we'll learn ways to turn these negative statements around in the next chapter!

1.

2.

3.

4.

5.

Chapter 4
Establishing a Positive Mindset

Upward and Downward Spirals

Establishing a positive body image is an important part of feeling good about who we are. Another important skill to learn is how to develop a positive *mental* self-image. Even though we may not walk down the street speaking out loud to ourselves, we *do* have an inner voice that influences our emotions and actions. By learning how to give ourselves encouraging messages, we can gain confidence and accomplish our goals more easily. When we encourage ourselves, we take ourselves on an "upward spiral," and when we put ourselves down we take a "downward spiral." In this chapter we will learn several ways to develop a positive mindset and take ourselves on an upward spiral. We will also learn some actions we can take to prevent our becoming too critical of ourselves.

Slumber Party

Sonya: If I laugh any more tonight I'm going to explode!

Caitlin: I doubt it . . . but you were laughing so hard you were snorting!

Amanda: You guys, we're all really silly tonight . . . . It feels really good, because I've been feeling kind of sad this week.

Trinecia: You didn't tell me that and I saw you every single day in science class!

Amanda: I know. I guess I felt bad about feeling sad, you know?

Sonya: What were you sad about?

Amanda: Well, a bunch of stuff. I said hi to Jeremy in the hall and he walked right past me like I was invisible. Then I just couldn't seem to understand the Spanish homework and I felt kind of stupid. Then I guess I started telling myself I was stupid and ugly.

Caitlin: Sounds like a downward spiral to me . . . like when you tell yourself something negative and it leads to another negative thought. I've had some days like that, when I tell myself I'm fat. But you know you're not stupid or ugly, Amanda, even if it feels like it sometimes. Neither am I.

Trinecia: Yeah, I know what you guys mean. When I catch myself going on a downward spiral like that I try to remind myself of some of the cool stuff that I've done before. Like that time I helped the second grade reading class, or the science fair award I won. Once I begin thinking of those things, I start feeling pretty good again.

Sonya: I do that trick too. It's like an upward spiral instead of a downward spiral. I also like to jump up and down on my bed for awhile. It makes me feel good.

Trinecia: Hey, great idea!

Everybody starts jumping on the bed and giggling out loud.

Sonya's Mom: *Girls!* . . . It's 2 A.M.. Aren't you asleep yet?

Sonya: Sorry, Mom. We were on an upward spiral!

Everybody giggles.

？？ Quiz Time ？？

Our outlook (the way we see situations and think about events in the world) can have a big impact on our self-image. Take this quiz to help you discover some of the positive and negative outlooks you might have about yourself right now. Do you usually take yourself on an upward or a downward spiral?

1. When I start to feel bad about myself, I usually:

A. Go hide in my closet and hope nobody finds me
B. Take time to think about every time I've ever failed in my life
C. Stop and think about some of my past accomplishments
D. Tell myself that I have a lot of great personal qualities to feel good about

2. My favorite thing about myself is:

A. What favorite thing? I don't have a favorite thing about myself
B. Hey, I'm not comfortable saying nice things about myself, okay?
C. I am smart, caring, and have a great sense of humor
D. I have some great talents like dancing, sports, etc.

3. If somebody asked me to describe myself, I would say that I am:

A. Kind of stupid

B. Just an okay person . . . nobody special

C. A nice person and a good listener

D. A strong, confident, smart girl

4. When I face a new challenge in my life (like learning a new skill or meeting new people) I usually tell myself that:

A. I don't think I can do this

B. I know I can't do this so I won't even try

C. I will do well because I'll give it my best

D. I'm a little bit nervous but I'll be okay because new challenges are exciting

5. Some of the positive things I can say to myself today are:

A. Forget positive things. I'm a total idiot!

B. I'm too depressed to say something nice to myself

C. I may not be perfect, but I'm pretty cool

D. I'm a smart, caring person

Answers

If you answered mostly As and Bs:

It's time to learn some new skills to pump yourself up! You've probably been spending a lot of energy taking yourself on a downward spiral. You might even think that it's conceited—or "stuck up"—to say nice things about yourself, but it's not. Practice saying one nice thing to yourself right now! Start by reading #5, answer C from the quiz you just took. Read it out loud, and say it three times. Good job! You can do this! And remember, if you're feeling really down, it's smart to ask for some help from a teacher, counselor, or other adult you trust. Keep reading this chapter, too, and you can learn some other ways to turn a downward spiral into an upward spiral. Good luck!

If you answered mostly Cs and Ds:

You already practice some good ways to take yourself on an upward spiral. Saying positive, encouraging things to yourself helps you to try new things and succeed at many tasks. Your self-confidence grows when you think positively. You probably know that nobody can do everything perfectly, so you remember to do your best and congratulate yourself for trying hard. You know that it's normal to feel down sometimes, but you don't stay down very long. Keep reading this chapter to get some other good ways to take yourself on an upward spiral. Good work!

Did You Know?

Keeping a Positive Attitude

Let's start learning some ways to have a good attitude. Read the facts listed below, and then at the bottom of the page circle or check off some of the ways that you could take care of yourself.

- In scientific studies, people who keep a journal have been shown to stay healthier than people who don't.
- Exercising—like walking, swimming, or dancing—can help people feel happy.
- Most people report that they talk to themselves. (Now if only we all learned to say *nice* things to ourselves, we'd be better off!)
- Talking to a friend can often make us feel better when we feel sad.
- Taking care of a pet can extend people's life expectancy.
- Sometimes when we help other people, we feel better ourselves.

Circle things that you might do to help lift your spirits when you feel down:

Remind myself of some of the great things I have already accomplished in my life.

Read a great book.

Think of a new personal project to get involved in.

Draw a picture expressing my feelings.

Ju_mp on a trampoline.

Write my feelings out in my journal.

Hang out with my friends and talk.

Take my dog for a long walk and talk to her about life.

Check It Out!

Losin' the Blues

On the list below, circle *all* of the things you could do if you were feeling blue.

Call my best friend to talk

Join a new club

Get help with homework at the tutoring clinic

Read an old favorite book

Do some laps around the track at school

Put on my favorite CD and sing along really loudly

Tell an adult who I trust about how I'm feeling and ask for suggestions

Tell <u>myself</u> that I'm smart, strong, and nice

Pet my cat/dog/gerbil/frog/fish (Well, maybe not my fish.)

Buy a new plant and take care of it

The Downward Spiral

First you begin to set unrealistic goals:
"I have to be liked by everyone."

Then you start to use more self-criticism:
*"I really messed up when I talked back to Tom, and now I'm afraid
of what my other friends will think."*

Next you begin to feel depressed or unhappy:
"I am sad because NOBODY likes me."

Then you use even more self-criticism:
*"I don't know how to be a good friend, I can't get along
with others, I'm not a very likable person."*

Finally you feel even more depressed or unhappy:
*"I hate myself for what I have done and
I'm really feeling depressed."*

Yikes! Time to turn it upside down!

Finally you feel better as a result.
*"I'm happy with almost all of my other
friendships and I can feel good about that."*

Next you shift from self-criticism to realistic and positive thoughts:
*"Even though Tom is mad at me it doesn't mean I am a bad person
or that I am not worth hanging around if I don't do what he says.
There are lots of good things about me as a friend."*

Then you set a realistic goal.
*"I want Tom to like me, but it's important for me to stick up for my
own thoughts and feelings."*

First you're feeling pretty low from the downward spiral you just took!
"I hate myself for what I have done and I'm really feeling depressed."

The Upward Spiral

I Should, I Have to, I Want to: What Works Best?

Sometimes, important people in our lives give us good advice. They might say things like, "You should try to do your best," or "You should be careful when you cross a busy street." These kinds of "should" statements are fine. But other times, we say "I should" statements to ourselves that set us up for a downward spiral. You see, some "I should" statements disguise unrealistic goals that we set for ourselves. Let's take a look at one example:

I should exercise every day.

Sounds okay, right? Well, not really. To get a better idea about why this "I should" statement might take us on a downward spiral, we can change the "I should" to an "I have to." The "I should" statement above, for example, changes to:

I have to exercise every day.

But is it really true that anybody "has to" exercise every day? Of course not! And if you tell yourself you should (or you have to) exercise every day, and then you miss a day, you might feel badly and start yourself on a downward spiral like this:

I should exercise every day.

I didn't exercise today.

I am a failure because I didn't exercise every day.

So how can we set goals that will take us on an upward spiral? Easy! We can use "I want to" statements instead of "I should" and "I have to" statements. See how different it sounds when we do this with the example sentence:

I should exercise every day.

I have to exercise every day.

I want to be healthy and fit, so I will try to exercise several times each week.

Okay!

Now this is a statement that will take you on an upward spiral because it is a goal that you can really reach.

Changing an "I Should" to an "I Want to"

Now it's time to change some "I should" statements into " I have to" statements (to see how silly they sound) and then change them into "I want" statements that will take us on the upward spiral.

I should get straight As in school.

I have to get straight As in school.

I want to do well in school, so I will try my best to get good grades.

I should do whatever my boyfriend wants me to.

I have to do whatever my boyfriend wants me to.

I want to get along with my boyfriend, but I have a mind of my own.

I should be nice to everybody all of the time.

I have to be nice to everybody all of the time.

I want to be a good person, but that doesn't mean I can please everybody.

Now it's time to change one of your own "I should" statements into an "I want" statement.

I should _____

I have to_____

I want to _____

Dear Suzie

Dear Suzie,

I am usually the kind of person who can make everybody, even myself, laugh. But I missed a block in the soccer game a couple of weeks ago, and it seems like ever since I've been having a really hard time. I feel like I can't concentrate on my homework, I'm tired after school, and when I try to sleep at night I just end up worrying about how I should be doing better. I'm starting to feel like I mess up at everything I do. I'm embarrassed to tell my friends how I feel. What should I do?

Blue in Biloxi

Dear Blue,

It sounds like you've been feeling depressed lately. Sometimes people feel depressed because of something that happens—like losing a good friend, or not doing very well at something we're usually good at, like blocking a goal in soccer, for example, or lots of other things. Sometimes people feel depressed because they think they have to be absolutely perfect at everything they do . . . and that just isn't possible. So when we make a normal, human mistake, we can be pretty hard on ourselves. It sounds like you're being pretty hard on yourself right now.

We all have times when we feel kind of blue. It's important to remind ourselves that we can't be perfect, but that we all have special talents and unique abilities. We need to encourage ourselves. And if you do that and still feel bad, it's good to talk to somebody you trust about how you're feeling. We all get the blues sometimes, but there are ways to pick ourselves up. Good Luck!

Suzie

Page

Things I'm Good At

Time to get creative. Get some old magazines (make sure you ask if it's okay to cut them up), scissors, and some glue or paste. Create a collage using words and pictures that you cut out. The theme of the collage is "Things I'm Good At." You might want to color in the edges with crayon or magic marker, add some glitter, or decorate and write any way that feels good. Next time you are feeling "blue" you can look at this page and it will help you remember things to celebrate about yourself.

Journal Assignment

Dating Interview

In this chapter we talked about what you can do to feel good about yourself. One way to feel good about yourself is to hook up with friends you can count on. In the next Go Grrrls section we're going to talk about friends, boys who are friends, and boyfriends, too.

Here is your journal assignment: Interview your mom, dad, aunt, guardian, or some other adult you like and trust. You can write down his or her answers in this book or you can record the interview if you have a tape recorder or video camera. If it makes it more fun, you can act like a TV news reporter during the interview. Have fun!

1. How old were you when you went on your first date?

2. How old do you think people should be when they go on their first date?

3. Do you think it's okay to date more than one person, or should someone date only one person at a time?

4. What do people do on a date?

5. Who should plan what to do on the date? Who should pay?

6. How should a person decide whom to go out with?

7. What made you want to go out on a date with somebody?

8. What did you feel like when you first started dating? (Were you excited, scared, happy, nervous, etc.?)

9. What do you think about guys and girls going out together in groups?

Chapter 5

Making and Keeping Friends

Friends are so important. Good friends can laugh and cry together, share their secrets, and just hang out. Friends can teach each other about new cultures and interests. They can also spend hours just talking about life's troubles and triumphs. Think about some of your friends. What qualities do they have that make them a good friend to you? In this chapter we will talk about what kind of friends to choose and what makes friends special. We will also learn some ways to meet new people, and ways to fix friendship problems with people we already know. We all need friends!

Slumber Party

Amanda: I'm so glad you could all sleep over tonight! At school yesterday, somebody asked me who my best friend is and I didn't really know what to say. I mean, we're all really good friends.

Sonya: Yeah, but sometimes you and Caitlin seem really close because you both play basketball. Other times you and Trinecia are like best friends because you both like drama class and acting. And sometimes you and I are like best friends because we both play guitar.

Caitlin: Yeah, we do kind of switch around with best friends. I'm just glad that I know all of you guys. I always feel like there is somebody I can talk to.

Trinecia: Shhhh. I'm *sleepy*, you guys!

Amanda: (whispering) Sorry. Yeah, I guess we all take care of each other in a way.

Caitlin: Yeah. And it's okay if we all feel like we have different best friends at different times. I just hate it when we don't get along with each other.

Trinecia: Shut up, okay? It's after 3 A.M.!

Caitlin: (whispering) Sorry, again, Trinecia.

Amanda: You know, even though we are good friends, sometimes we just get mad at each other still. Like that time—remember, Sonya?—when you told everybody that I liked Sean White? I was raged out!

Sonya: Oh, no. I was hoping that you forgot about that. Yeah, I'm sorry. I didn't mean to tell your secret. I don't even remember who I said something to. I'm just glad that we worked it out.

Caitlin: How did you guys work it out?

Amanda: Well, Sonya put a friendship bracelet in my locker, with a really nice card that said she missed me.

Trinecia: All right, you guys. I give up on sleeping. Now I'm totally awake. (She sits up and rubs her eyes.) Before I met all of you, I used to hang out with this one girl—Melissa—and she was just bad news. She started shoplifting at the mall when I was with her, and all kinds of crazy stuff. I tried to stay her friend, but she never listened to me. Plus, I was afraid she would get me in trouble.

Sonya: Yeah, sometimes you can solve friendship problems . . . but sometimes you can't. I guess you just have to try to talk things out and then trust your instincts.

Amanda: My instincts say that I'm really glad you are all my friends.

Trinecia: Yeah, me too . . . even if you *did* wake me up at 3 A.M.! But because you're my friends, I forgive you. And as long as we're all awake, let's make up a special handshake that only we will know.

Everybody: Let's do it!

? ? Quiz Time ? ?

There are two copies of this quiz because one is for you and one is for a friend of yours! You can even make some more copies and take the quiz over and over with all of your friends. There are no answers for this quiz because only you and your friend can supply the answers. Have fun!

1. My friend's favorite

color is_____.

movie is _____.

song is _____.

subject at school is _____.

2. If my friend could choose one of these foods for dinner, she would choose:

a. Peanut butter and jelly

b. Steamed veggies
c. Pizza
d. A burrito
e. Macaroni and cheese

3. My friend's birthday is on _____.

4. The thing my friend would *least* like to do on this list is:

a. Give a piano recital
b. Stay at a quiet cabin with no TV for a week
c. Write an essay about her favorite music group
d. Give a speech in front of the whole school

5. My friend would say that *my* best characteristic is:

a. I'm kind
b. I'm funny
c. I'm smart
d. I'm talented

6. I'd say that my friend's best characteristic is:

a. She's kind
b. She's funny
c. She's smart
d. She's talented

7. If my best friend could choose to be one of these animals, she would be a:

a. Giraffe, because _____.

b. Panther, because _____.

c. Dalmatian, because _____.

d. Chimpanzee, because _____.

1. My friend's favorite

color is_____.

movie is _____.

song is _____.

subject at school is _____.

2. If my friend could choose one of these foods for dinner, she would choose:

a. Peanut butter and jelly

b. Steamed veggies

c. Pizza

d. A burrito

e. Macaroni and cheese

3. My friend's birthday is on _____.

4. The thing my friend would *least* like to do on this list is:

a. Give a piano recital

b. Stay at a quiet cabin with no TV for a week

c. Write an essay about her favorite music group

d. Give a speech in front of the whole school

5. My friend would say that *my* best characteristic is:

a. I'm kind

b. I'm funny

c. I'm smart

d. I'm talented

6. I'd say that my friend's best characteristic is:

a. She's kind

b. She's funny

c. She's smart

d. She's talented

7. If my best friend could choose to be one of these animals, she would be a:

a. Giraffe, because _____.

b. Panther, because _____.

c. Dalmatian, because _____.

d. Chimpanzee, because _____.

Did You Know?

What Makes a Good Friend?

Think about some of your friends. What qualities do they have that make them a good friend to you? To help you find out what makes your friends so special, fill in the blanks on this page!

My friend _____ is special because (she/he) is _____,
           (your friend's name)   (one positive quality)

_____, and _____. Some of the interests that
  (another positive quality)   (another positive quality)

we have in common are _____ and _____.
                   (one interest you share)   (another interest you share)

One new thing that I learned about from being friends with her/him is how to _____

_____. One of my favorite times with her/him was when
(something new that you do, think, feel, or like)

_____
(a time when you really had fun together or really helped each other out)

_____.

Now that you have filled in the blanks above, answer the following questions:

1. Is popularity one of the most important qualities of a friend? Why or why not?

2. What three qualities do you think *your* friends would say make *you* a good friend? Why?

Make It Happen

Make a Friend

Sometimes it's hard to make new friends, but we learn so much from friends that it's important to reach out to new people. Is there somebody in one of your classes at school or someone in your neighborhood whom you think is really nice but you don't know very well yet? Here is an action plan for you to try to get to know that person better. You can make it happen!

My New Friend Game Plan

1. My potential new friend's name is _____.

2. I usually see her/him at _____.
(where and when)

3. I think she/he is interested in _____.
(sports, music, studying, etc.)

4. Some things I think we might have in common are _____.
(go to the same school, both like hip-hop, etc.)

5. When I introduce myself to her/him I can suggest that we meet sometime to _____

_____.
(study together, play basketball, go to a movie, go to the mall, have dinner at my house, etc.)

6. I will try to get to know my potential new friend better on _____.
(Monday morning, Sunday afternoon, etc.)

Congratulations! Now you have a plan, so it's time to make it happen! Good luck!

My Friendship Want Ad

Think about the qualities that are important for a friend to have. Then write a want ad that includes these qualities. Here is an example of a want ad:

Seeking a new friend: I am looking for somebody to talk with and go Rollerblading with. I'd like someone who is friendly, outgoing, and funny. I think a friend is someone who you can tell secrets to, so I have to trust you. We could talk on the phone for hours, about school, friends, guys, and life!

My Response to the Friendship Want Ad

Write a response to the friendship want ad that you received. In your response, answer the other person, and think about the qualities you would bring to the friendship. For example:

My response to the friendship ad: I am a very active person and I would enjoy Rollerblading and other outdoor activities, like hiking and swimming. I agree with you about wanting a friend you can trust . . . that's so important! In the past I've had friends who I trusted, but they told my other friends things I didn't want shared. I like to talk a lot, so we could talk on the phone about all kinds of things. Let's meet and we can see what happens.

I Am a Friend

I am a friend

I share my thoughts and feelings with people I care about

I give others the gifts of caring and sharing

I am a friend

I let other people share their thoughts and feelings with me

I let them give me the gifts of caring and sharing

I know that friendships take time to grow

For a rose to bloom it needs water, sunlight, and time

For a friendship to grow, it needs work, patience, and care

I am a friend

I listen, I learn, I love

Every new friendship I make gives me a chance to learn and grow

I am a friend

Dear Suzie

Dear Suzie,

I really like my new friend Anne, but sometimes I feel weird when I visit her house. I ate dinner there last week and her family said Grace before they ate. I didn't know what to do because my family has never done that. Then we had artichokes on our salad. I never tasted them before and I couldn't decide if I thought they were really good or really gross. Also, they played some strange jazzy music while we ate. I really like Anne a lot, but I'm kind of afraid to ask her to eat over at my house now. What should I do?

Indigestion in Indiana

Dear Indigestion,

You are so lucky! One thing that friends do for us is teach us about different ways of living. Every family is unique and when you get to be old enough (like you are now) you get to explore the different customs, cultures, habits, and interests of your friends and their families. I bet your friend will be a little nervous about visiting your family too. She might find your family's habits strange. That's normal! But it's also exciting to explore the world of new friends in your life. This is a great opportunity for you and your friend to talk about your differences and your similarities. Have a good time!

Suzie

Page

True Friends

It's paste-up time again. The theme of this work of art is going to be "True Friends." Find some photographs of you and your friends (or maybe you can take some photos especially for this page). You can use the photographs the way they are, or you can cut them into interesting shapes before you paste them on the page. In between photos, write words that describe important friendship qualities (like "trust" or "fun"). It's your masterpiece, so decorate the images any way you like!

Journal Assignment

Friendship Friction

Good friends are so important. Friendship brings us fun, new interests, people who care about us, and people we can care about. But have you ever had an argument with a friend? Of course! Sometimes we disagree with our friends, misunderstandings happen, and before you know it you're not sure if you are still friends at all. Your journal assignment is to write about one time that you had a problem (or a fight) with a friend. What did you fight about? Who started the fight? Did you make up? If so, how did you make up? (If you are attending a Go Grrrls club right now, make sure that you write about somebody who *isn't* in the club.)

Journal Assignment

Two Medium-Sized Problems

We have been talking about how important it is to have friends. We know that friends help us celebrate good times and work through hard times. We all need friends, but it is really important to be able to rely on ourselves, too. In the next Go Grrrls chapter we'll learn about Independence. Being independent means you can make choices for yourself, but this takes some practice. If we want more freedom to make choices, we have to accept more responsibility for ourselves and our actions, too. One way to begin to be more independent is to learn how to solve problems in a responsible way. Your journal assignment is to write down two problems that you have run into this year. These should be real problems, but not really, really serious problems. Here are two examples of the kind of problem we want you to write down:

- *My friends all say that I should go to this party next weekend, but I know the guy's parents aren't going to be home and I don't know what to do.*
- *I'm having a really hard time with social studies and there's a test next week. I'm nervous about it but I'm not sure what to do.*

Here are two examples of problems that are very important but are too serious to use for our next club activity or for you to solve on your own. (We'll talk about these kinds of problems a little later on, in chapter 9.)

- *My mom is drinking all the time and I'm getting really scared.*
- *My grandfather just died and I'm so sad.*

Okay, time to write down two medium-sized problems to work on:

1.

2.

Chapter 6

Establishing Independence through Problem Solving

Being independent means making more choices for yourself, which takes some practice. If we want more freedom to make choices, we have to accept more responsibility for ourselves and our actions, too. One way to begin to be more independent is to learn how to solve simple problems in a responsible way.

Slumber Party

Trinecia: It seems like a long time since we had our first slumber party over here at my house.

Caitlin: Yeah . . . we know each other so much better now than we did then.

Amanda: That's for sure. I even know all of your favorite colors, favorite music, and the guys you like at school.

Sonya: You keep quiet about that last one, now!

Amanda: I will, I will!

Trinecia: Speaking of keeping quiet about something . . . I have a problem that I want you guys to help me figure out.

Sonya: What's up? Are you okay?

Trinecia: Yeah, I'm okay. It's not a really big problem, just a decision I need to make. You know that guy Sam that I've been eyeing for a little while?

Caitlin: How could we *not* know about him? You talk about him all the time!

Trinecia: I know, I know. Well, he asked me to meet him in the library after school on Monday.

Amanda: Honey, that doesn't sound like a problem to me!

Trinecia: No, but I said I would do it, and then I remembered that I have basketball practice on Monday after school.

Sonya: Whoops! So what are you going to do?

Trinecia: That's what I want to talk to you guys about. I really want to go meet him, but you know that basketball is important to me. Besides, my coach will kill me if she finds out I cut practice.

Amanda: Not to mention what your mom will do to you!

Trinecia: Yeah, my mom always wants to know where I am.

Sonya: I know! Let's try to think of every single thing you could do. But there is one rule: We can't say whether they are "good" or "bad" ideas until we finish the whole list. Then you can decide which one is the best thing to try.

Amanda: Yeah, let's see how many things we can come up with.

Trinecia: Okay. I'll go get some paper to write them down on.

The girls all take turns writing down their ideas. Then they hand the list to Trinecia, who reads it aloud.

Trinecia: Wow, you guys came up with a lot of possibilities! Okay let's hear . . . I could:

Blow off basketball practice and go meet Sam.

Meet Sam first and tell him that I forgot about practice but I need to go. And then ask if we can meet on Tuesday instead.

Ditch Sam and go to practice.

Go to practice, tell the coach I feel sick, and then secretly go meet Sam at the library.

Go meet Sam and ask him if he wants to come watch me practice.

Skip practice *and* ditch Sam. Go home and talk to the cat instead.

Call Sam over the weekend to tell him that I spaced out about practice. Ask if he can meet me another time.

On Monday morning, go tell the coach that I will be a half hour late to practice because I scheduled something else by mistake. Ask her if that would be a problem.

Quit basketball because it might spoil other times I could meet guys.

Quit liking guys because they take too much time to worry about.

Ask Sam to join the girls' basketball team so we can be together a lot.

Trinecia: Hey, you guys are pretty good! This list actually really helps—even the silly ideas . . . . at least they made me laugh!

Sonya: My sister taught me that trick, about listing all of your choices without judging them until they're all written down.

Caitlin: That's a great trick. Of course, you still have to figure out what's good and what's bad about the possibilities *after* you list them.

Trinecia: That's a fact. Like that idea about asking my coach if I could show up late for practice. It sounds like a great idea, but you don't know Ms. Smallshaw! No way would she let me be late!

Amanda: So what do you think you're going to do, Trinecia?

Trinecia: I think I'll call Sam tomorrow to tell him that I messed up . . . and I'll ask him if he can meet me on Tuesday instead.

Sonya: That sounds good. What if he says no?

Caitlin: Hey, girlfriend, if he says no, then he isn't worth meeting anyway!

They all laugh and Trinecia and Caitlin give each other a high five.

Quiz Time

Take this quiz to help you think about the ways you sometimes try to solve problems.

1. Problem solving:

A. isn't very important because I never have any problems
B. is depressing, because who wants to talk about problems anyway?
C. only matters in math class
D. is a really useful skill to have

2. When I have a problem to solve, I usually:

A. ignore it and hope that it will go away
B. wait until the last possible minute and then do something quickly, without thinking about it
C. let somebody else make a decision for me
D. try to imagine all of the possible solutions, then choose the best one

3. Problem solving can only be used in situations where:

A. things have gotten really bad
B. you'll get in trouble if you don't come up with a solution
C. somebody wants you to do something different
D. you have an awareness that there is a problem

4. If a friend came to me with a difficult problem I would tell her to:

A. keep her problems to herself
B. decide what to do by saying "eenie meenie minie mo"
C. forget about the problem and just eat some ice cream instead
D. sit down with her and try to think of as many possible solutions as we could

Answers

If you answered A, B, or C to any of the questions you still have some skills to learn before you'll be a good problem solver! The answers in choice D to the questions reflect some of the important aspects of problem solving. First of all, problem solving is a skill—something all people can get better at if they practice. Yes, that includes your parents! The most critical part of the skill is recognizing you have a problem and thinking of as many solutions as you can. Just practice, choose a day and try to think of multiple solutions to the problems you experience for that day.

Did You Know?

The Five Steps to Solving Problems

The key to learning how to make decisions or solve problems is to know the steps to take. Remember, for serious problems it's always a good idea to seek help from someone you trust. Here are the problem solving steps:

1. Define the problem:

What is the problem? It's a good idea to write it down. Keep it as short as you can. For example, in the slumber party sample problem, how would you define the problem? (Example: Trinecia wants to play basketball and meet Sam, but can't do both at once.)

2. Brainstorm choices:

The next step is to think of all the possible choices you could make to solve the problem. It's a good idea to write down as many as you can think of, and make sure you let yourself come up with some silly or outrageous choices, too! *One rule during this step is that you don't eliminate any choice or criticize any idea.* The slumber party girls did a really good job at this. Review their list to see how this is done.

3. Evaluate the choices:

This is the part where you figure out the pros and cons of each choice. It might help to put a + or - next to your brainstormed ideas. What are some of the pros and cons of each of the slumber party girls' ideas?

4. Make your decision:

Now that we've evaluated the ideas, it's time to select the best idea from the list. Which one do you think would be best for you? Put your initials next to the idea that you think works the best on the slumber party girls' list.

5. If your decision isn't working out, start back at number 1!!!

The last step is to keep an eye on how your decision is working for you. You might need to go back to the beginning. . . or, your decision might work out really great! Either way, give yourself a pat on the back for learning the art of problem solving!

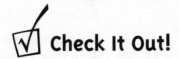 **Check It Out!**

Actions and Consequences

You have a math test next week but you don't understand the material in the chapter you are working on. Check all of the ways you might act if this was happening. Next, put a star next to any of the ways you think would be the best ways to act if this was happening.

Drop out of math and never take another math class again ever, ever, ever.

Act like you understand because you are embarrassed about not getting it.

Ask one of your friends to let you cheat on the test.

Fake being sick on the day of the test so you don't have to take it.

Take the test and just make up numbers for answers. Who cares about math anyway?

Go to the math tutoring session after school.

Ask the teacher for extra help.

Set aside extra study time for math so you can really try to figure it out.

Ask one of your friends to help you with your home-work.

Problem solving skills are important to learn because they help us make good choices. The choices we make and actions we take can affect our lives in many important ways. Sometimes our actions have consequences (results) that can last the rest of our lives. There are two lists below. On the left side is a list of actions, and on the right side is a list of consequences. Draw a line connecting the action on the left with the consequence that *might* follow on the right.

Actions	Consequences
You decide to postpone having sex until you are much older.	You get drunk, throw up on your new shirt, and make a fool of yourself. You are embarrassed to go to school on Monday.
You cheat on a social studies test.	You get to be so good that you start your own band and actually get some paying gigs by the time you're in high school.
You overhear someone putting down a girl at school whom you think is pretty nice, and you stick up for her out loud.	You find out that you have an STD (sexually transmitted disease) and have to go to a clinic for treatment and tell your boyfriend to do the same.
You decide to drink beer at a Friday night party.	You feel good about respecting yourself, and because you waited, you have a chance to accomplish many goals and dreams that you couldn't have if you had become a teen mom.
Your boyfriend and you get carried away and have unprotected sex.	The principal catches you and you get suspended.
You decide to practice your electric guitar for one hour every night after you finish your homework.	She hears about what you did and invites you to come on her family's upcoming skiing vacation.
A girl in the hall says something nasty about your outfit so you call her a *#%$! and step on her toes really hard.	Because she is so impressed with your actions, and she likes your new friend, your mom actually drives you both to the mall the next week.
Your mom doesn't want you to go to the mall with your new friend, so you invite your friend to your house and make sure your mom has a chance to get to know her better.	Your classroom teacher catches you, calls your parents, and you get an F for the class.

As you can see from this exercise, actions do have consequences and many of them are really bad consequences. One of the reasons people get into trouble is that they forget to think about consequences. For instance, if you have unprotected sex you could get pregnant *and* get a STD (sexually transmitted disease)—that's what I call a consequence! It's important to think about what you do and what could happen as a result of your actions.

Now color each positive action and consequence pair (the ones where something cool happened as a result of the action) in a matching color, until you have a pretty rainbow of positive action/consequence pairs.

Making Decisions and Solving Problems

Use this form to help you solve a problem of your own. You can write on this page, but make copies of the form on the next page so you can use the form over and over again.

Here are the steps you can use:

1. Define the problem. (What is it?)
2. Brainstorm choices. (Think of every possible solution—even silly ones! Don't criticize any of them yet!)
3. Evaluate the choices. (What are the pros and cons of each choice?)
4. Make your decision. (Select the best idea.)
5. If your decision doesn't work out, start over again at #1!

1. Define the problem.

The problem is:

_____

_____

2. Brainstorm choices.

I could:

3. Evaluate the choices.

Put a + and - beside each idea. What is positive about that choice? What is negative?

1.	+:	-:
2.	+:	-:
3.	+:	-:
4.	+:	-:
5.	+:	-:
6.	+:	-:
7.	+:	-:
8.	+:	-:
9.	+:	-:
10.	+:	-:

4. Make your decision.

I decided to _____ because _____.

5. If your decision doesn't work out, start back at #1 and try another idea!

Making Decisions and Solving Problems

Use this form to help you solve a problem of your own.

Here are the steps you can use:

1. Define the problem. (What is it?)
2. Brainstorm choices. (Think of every possible solution—even silly ones! Don't criticize any of them yet!)
3. Evaluate the choices. (What are the pros and cons of each choice?)
4. Make your decision. (Select the best idea.)
5. If your decision doesn't work out, start over again at #1!

1. Define the problem.

The problem is:

_____

_____

2. Brainstorm choices.	**3. Evaluate the choices.**
I could:	Put a + and - beside each idea. What is positive about that choice? What is negative?

1.	+:	-:
2.	+:	-:
3.	+:	-:
4.	+:	-:
5.	+:	-:
6.	+:	-:
7.	+:	-:
8.	+:	-:
9.	+:	-:
10.	+:	-:

4. Make your decision.

I decided to _____ because _____.

5. If your decision doesn't work out, start back at #1 and try another idea!

Journal Assignment

Speaking Up

Here are some questions for you: Have you ever known the answer to your science teacher's question but you didn't raise your hand to speak? Have you ever heard somebody spread mean gossip about someone you know but you didn't say anything? Have you ever heard somebody telling a racist joke but you didn't speak up against it? Did you ever want to return a shirt to a store but changed your mind because you didn't want to hassle with the clerk?

For this journal assignment, write about one time when *you wish you had spoken up* for yourself or someone else but didn't. If you can't think of a time like that, write about a time when you *did* speak up and felt good about it.

Chapter 7
Establishing Independence through Assertiveness

Assertiveness is an important skill to learn if we are to become more independent. Being assertive means that you respect your rights and feelings *and* you respect other people's rights and feelings, too. In this chapter you will learn new skills to make sure you can speak up for yourself.

Slumber Party

Sonya: Friday! Friday! Friday! My day! Friday!

Trinecia: You are all wound up, Sonya.

Amanda: You are, girl. You're acting totally gay.

Sonya: No way! I am not! I'm just happy it's the weekend.

Amanda: You are so! Isn't she acting completely gay, you guys?

Trinecia: Absolutely.

Caitlin: Well, actually . . . she *is* being fun and silly, but I have to tell you that it makes me feel bad when you call that "gay."

Amanda: C'mon, Caitlin, you know what I mean. Everybody says that just to mean that somebody's acting geeky.

Caitlin: Yeah, and that's the problem. I never told you guys this, but my aunt Vickie is a lesbian. She's one of my favorite people of all time, and it hurts when I hear somebody use the word "gay" like it's something bad.

Trinecia: I hear you. Sorry about that, Caitlin. I guess we just weren't thinking.

Amanda: Yeah, I'm sorry, too. I didn't really mean anything by it, but I guess I just didn't think about how that could hurt somebody.

Caitlin: That's okay you guys. I'm just glad I spoke my mind.

Sonya: Yeah, I'm proud of you for telling us how you really felt.

Trinecia: Me, too, Caitlin. That took some nerve.

Caitlin: Thanks, you guys. Lately, I've been trying to practice being assertive—you know, when you respect yourself and your own opinions and you also respect other people's opinions. I used to just be quiet and not speak up, but I'm learning that it feels good to stand up for myself and my beliefs.

Amanda: You go girl!

Sonya: Yes you do. But it's still Friday, my day! Friday, my day!

Amanda: Sonya, you are so . . . Goofy!

Sonya: Thank you very much!

They all laugh.

Did You Know?

Styles of Communication

There are three main styles of communication. Read the definitions of these three styles below and think about what your main style is right now.

Assertive:

Being assertive means that you say what you think, feel, want, or believe in a way that isn't mean or disrespectful to another person. You stand up for your own rights and treat other people with respect.

Passive:

When you act passively, you don't respect your own right to express your ideas, needs, wants, feelings, and opinions. Sometimes people act passively because they are afraid to risk the consequences if they say how they really feel. Sometimes people act passively because they don't know how to speak up for themselves. Being passive might help you avoid a conflict in the short term, but in the long run it can cause you bigger problems. You might feel like other people are taking advantage of you.

Aggressive:

When you act aggressively, you disregard another person's right to be respected. An aggressive response is one that is mean, hurtful, or a put-down. You might get what you want in the short term, but in the long run you might make other people really angry and cause bigger problems for yourself later.

Now that you know what these words mean, let's find out more about being assertive.

? ? Quiz Time ? ?

Read the paragraphs below. For each situation, circle the answer that matches what you would probably do. Try to identify which responses are assertive, aggressive, or passive.

1. You ride the school bus every day. There is a girl from your math class who rides the bus, too. She was really nice to you in class last week, and helped you figure out some of the mysteries of algebra. But she dresses kind of weird, and all the kids think her hair looks really stupid. On the bus on the way home, some friends of yours start pointing at her and giggling. One of them says to you, "Hey, check out that hair! She looks like a tornado hit her today!" You respond by:

A. Saying, "Oh yeah, well you look like a chihuahua yourself, so I wouldn't talk!"
B. Not saying anything . . . just nodding your head in silent agreement.
C. Saying, "Actually, her name is Nicki, and I don't care what her hair looks like . . . She's really nice and smart and she just helped me with my math homework."

2. Your science teacher, Ms. White, explains the procedure for the lab experiment. You are not sure whether she said to put two or three of the chemicals together. She is kind of loud and intimidating. You:

A. Say, "Hey, Ms. White! Why don't you try giving some decent instructions for a change!"
B. Don't say anything. You just mix the chemicals together and hope that you don't blow anything up.
C. Raise your hand and say, "Ms. White, could you please repeat those instructions? I didn't hear which of the chemicals to mix together."

3. You have a friend who always likes to decide what you are going to do on the weekend. She is mostly pretty nice, even though she is kind of pushy. On Friday in the cafeteria, she says to you, "I've got our weekend all planned out. We're going to rent a video. You'll sleep over at my house tonight, and we'll learn to French braid each other's hair." You really wanted to go bowling with some other friends. You:

A. Say, "Listen Miss Bossy-Pants-of-the-Century! I am getting sick and tired of you always telling me what to do! I'm going bowling and you can braid your own stupid hair."
B. You shake your head a little bit, but you don't want to hurt her feelings, so you just say okay. You decide to go bowling some other time.
C. Say, "Thank you for the offer, but I already planned to go bowling with some other people. Would you like to come with us?"

Answers

For each situation above there were three types of answers given: aggressive, passive, and assertive. If you answered mostly As, then you were acting aggressively. If you answered mostly Bs, then you were acting passively. If you answered mostly Cs, then you were acting assertively.

Make It Happen

Circle or check off all the things you could do to practice being assertive.

Ask a teacher to repeat confusing instructions for an assignment.

Tell a pushy friend that you don't want to do something.

Write a letter to the editor of a newspaper to "stand up" for a cause you believe in.

Raise your hand in a class where you don't usually talk a lot.

Talk to your principal about how students could get involved in improving the school.

Practice using simple refusal skills by looking in the mirror and saying things like: "No thank you. I'm not into that. I don't want to, thanks."

If you usually use an aggressive style, practice listening carefully to people before you respond.

Assertive, Aggressive, or Passive?

Introduction to situation #1

Okay, let's face it, sometimes you just can't help daydreaming about some cute guy. It can be hard, sometimes, to stick up for your rights when you get kind of weak in the knees every time you see him. It's really important, though, to be able to stick up for yourself, and stay out of risky situations. Let's see what happens in this situation.

Situation #1

A guy you really like invites you over to his house on a night when his parents aren't home. You think he's the greatest, and you'd like to go out with him, sometime, but you don't think it's a good idea to go to his house without his parents there.

Guy: Hey, do you wanna come over Friday night? My folks are going into town for the night, and I thought we could just hang out and stuff.

Girl #1: I really like you a lot, and I want to go out with you. Let's hang at my house.

Girl #2: Are you too stupid to live or what? I can't do that!

Girl #3: Well, I'm not supposed to do that, but I guess I could come for a little while.

Which response is assertive? Which one is passive? Which one is aggressive? Here is a little reminder of what each word means:

Assertive:

Being assertive means that you say what you think, feel, want, or believe in a way that isn't mean or disrespectful to another person. You stand up for your own rights and treat other people with respect.

Passive:

When you act passively, you don't respect your own right to express your ideas, needs, wants, feelings, and opinions. Sometimes people act passively because they are afraid to risk the consequences if they say how they really feel. Sometimes people act passively because they don't know how to speak up for themselves. Being passive might help you avoid a conflict in the short term, but in the long run it can cause you bigger problems. You might feel like other people are taking advantage of you.

Aggressive:

When you act aggressively, you disregard another person's right to be respected. An aggressive response is one that is mean, hurtful, or a put-down. You might get what you want in the short term, but in the long run you might make other people really angry and cause bigger problems for yourself later.

If you answered "I really like you a lot, and I want to go out with you. Let's hang at my house," you selected the assertive response. This communicates how you feel but isn't disrespectful. If you answered, "Are you too stupid to live or what?" you resorted to name calling and being disrespectful, which is aggressive. And if you answered, "Well, I'm not supposed to do that, but I guess I could come for a little while," you were being passive, because you did not respect your own desires.

Introduction to situation #2

Sometimes the hardest time to be assertive is when we are with people whose feelings and opinions we really value a lot. When a girl and a guy really like each other, they might feel very tempted to have sex. It is important to practice what to do in a situation like this before it happens.

Situation #2

You have been dating a guy for about 6 months. You really like him a lot and you know he really likes you, too. In fact, one day while you are kissing each other behind the football stadium after school, he tells you that he loves you and he's sure that some day you guys are going to get married. He tells you that if you really care for him you will "go all the way."

Guy: Maria, I really love you. Someday you're going to be my wife. I've been thinking. Wouldn't it really show how much we love each other if we made love?

Girl #1: Oh, Jeremy, that's so romantic. I don't know though. You really love me, right?

Girl #2: You absolute, incredible moron of a human being!

Girl #3: Jeremy, I care about you a lot. That's why it's really important to me that we wait. Let's go find everybody else and cool off.

Which response is assertive? Which one is passive? Which one is aggressive?

Dear Suzie

Dear Suzie,

I am in the 7th grade and I keep having trouble with an 8th grader named Wendy. She is really mean and she likes to tease kids. She keeps bothering me lately. Last week she tripped me in the hall and I dropped my books everywhere. I didn't get hurt, but it really made me mad. I already talked to one of my teachers about Wendy and he said that she is a problem and I should avoid her . . . but I can't because my locker is right by hers! What can I do?

Tromped On in Tucson

Dear Tromped On,

It seems like every school has a few bullies. A bully is someone who hurts or picks on someone else. Usually a bully does this to feel like she or he has power over other people. Studies show that a lot of bullies have been abused, themselves. They may not know any other way to act. Bullies use an aggressive style almost all the time.

There are a lot of different things you could try to stop Wendy (or anybody else) from bullying you.

- Talk to an adult you trust.
- Go to a safe place whenever you see the bully.
- Tell the bully to leave you alone.
- Avoid the bully as much as possible.
- Try to be with other people whenever the bully is near.

You already know that there is no magic solution, because you have tried talking to an adult. Here is a hint: You will probably have to keep trying all of these strategies. Talk to another teacher or the school counselor or vice principal. Ask if you can have your locker moved so that you can avoid Wendy more easily. Tell her, using your best assertive style, to leave you alone, but do this when you are in a safe place with other friends around. The most important thing is for you to stay safe and still stick up for yourself. Good luck.

Suzie

Journal Assignment

My Questions about Sex

In this chapter we talked about speaking up for yourself. It is important to understand that you have a right to be heard and that being assertive (not aggressive or passive) is the best way to get your message across. In the next chapter, we'll learn about sexuality. Sometimes it can be hard to be assertive, to speak up, and to ask questions about sex. But it's really important to understand our bodies!

Your journal assignment is to write down at least three questions, tales, or rumors you've heard about sex. If you are in a Go Grrrls club right now, your group leaders will answer your questions at the next meeting. If you are not, be assertive and take your questions to your doctor, the school nurse, your parents, your aunt, or some other adult that you trust.

Remember that even though some teenagers pretend they know everything about sex, they probably don't. While it's a good idea to talk to your friends about sexuality, don't rely on them for information about sex. They may give you some incorrect information!

Now write down at least three questions, tales, or rumors you've heard about sex.

1.

2.

3.

4.

5.

Chapter 8
Let's Talk About Sex

Are you curious about sex? It's natural to be curious! When we talk about sex, we aren't just talking about sexual intercourse. Sometimes people forget that sexuality also includes things like holding hands, kissing, and hugging. The topic of sex is complex. There is so much information to learn. We need to understand how our bodies work, of course, but that's not nearly enough to know about sex. We also need to think about our attitudes, beliefs, feelings, and behaviors when it comes to sexuality. In this chapter we will cover some basic information about sexuality. Remember, though, that this is a big subject so you will probably need to get more information from adults that you trust.

The very first thing to remember is that everybody's body changes at its own pace. Don't worry if you seem to be "ahead" or "behind" other girls' development. Your body will figure out what it needs to do.

Slumber Party

Caitlin: Since this is my slumber party, girls, I say that tonight's topic is sex, S-E-X.

Trinecia: Yeah, go girl. I can see you have sex on your mind.

Sonya: No tape recorders, please . . . .

Amanda: Well, here's my thing: I want to be in control when I have sex. I want to decide that this is what I want to do. At my sister's party I heard some girls talking about when they had sex for the first time. It sounded like it just kind of happened. Like they kind of wanted to but kind of didn't want to, but they did it anyway.

Sonya: Yeah, I know some girls and guys who have had sex already, and they say they weren't really ready. One friend of my cousin said she did it because her boyfriend said, "I'm going to dump you unless we do it."

Trinecia: That is *so* not cool. But it's not just guys who put on the pressure to have sex. I know this girl from my old school who did it, and then she was like, "I did it, so what are you waiting for?" It was like she was pressuring me to do it with somebody so she'd have company!

Caitlin: Yeah, but that's not us. Let's agree that each one of us needs to make up her own mind about sex—whether to do it or not.

Sonya: I agree, Caitlin, but sometimes it's hard to stop. I mean, I just had my first kiss last year, and I was all, "This is great but kind of gross, too." Now I'm all, "This is definitely great!" And I'm curious about what everything else would feel like, you know?

Caitlin: I know, I'm curious, too. But one other thing I know is that I really need to think about this and not do something that I might regret later.

Amanda: Yeah . . . like end up with a baby or get an STD. That would be such a major drag.

Caitlin: That would be. But it's not just about that. I just don't think I could trust anybody enough to go too far, yet.

Trinecia: That's so smart, Caitlin.

Sonya: Yeah, but you guys, it feels really good to make out with somebody. I didn't tell you about this yet, but this friend of my brother was over at our house last week after school while my mom was still at work, and, well . . .

Amanda: What, what, what?

Sonya: Well, we didn't "do it," if that's what you think . . . but I did kind of let him do more than just kiss me. He didn't stop to ask me. He just sort of started to take off my shirt, and it was scary but exciting, so . . .

Caitlin: Wow, Sonya. Isn't your brother in high school?

Sonya: Yeah, and so is this guy.

Trinecia: Just be careful, Sonya. My mom told me that most teenage girls who get pregnant were with a guy a lot older than they were. Older guys can put a lot more pressure on you.

Sonya: I didn't go all the way, you guys! Man!

Caitlin: We heard you, but we're just watching out for each other. You know, even though I personally think it's smart to wait until we're much older, let's all agree that if we *did* go all the way, we'd respect ourselves enough to be safe . . . meaning that we would use condoms and stuff.

Amanda: Right. Like I'm gonna go buy condoms at the drugstore. No way! The clerk there knows my whole family!

Sonya: Yeah, but you can go to a drugstore that you don't usually go to. Or you can go to Planned Parenthood. They have people there who will talk to you about safe sex and birth control and stuff.

Trinecia: How do you know that?

Sonya: My mom actually took me there once. She said it was good to know where to go, even though she wishes that I'll wait and be abstinent.

Caitlin: That means not doing it, right?

Sonya: Right.

Trinecia: Well, I say let's all pledge to respect ourselves and protect ourselves. What do you say?

Everybody: Yeah!

Questions and Answers about Sex

Some questions other Go Grrrls like you have asked:

What is puberty? I mean, what happens to make our bodies develop? Excellent question! Puberty begins in girls because of an increase in the body's production of female sex hormones. The names of these hormones are estrogen (pronounced "ess-tro-jen") and progesterone (pronounced "pro-jes-ter-own"). These hormones usually begin to increase when a girl is around 10 or 11 years old. Now, that doesn't mean that the whole process of maturing is finished then! It's just beginning. Some changes that you will notice include:

- Underarm and pubic hair begin to grow.
- Perspiration may increase.
- Breasts begin to develop.
- Hips become rounded.
- Eventually, menstrual periods begin.

What is a period? When will I get my first period? How long does it last? Another excellent question! Getting your period is one part of your body's menstrual cycle. The whole cycle usually takes about 28 days, but it can be longer or shorter (usually anywhere from 22 days up to 40 days!). A period usually lasts between 3 and 7 days.

The basic thing that happens is this: Once you mature, your body releases about one egg per month from one of your ovaries. Your uterus grows thick with a blood-rich lining every month just in case a fertilized egg comes by! If the egg does not get fertilized (no sperm meets the egg), it moves through your fallopian tube and into the uterus, where it starts to disintegrate. Because there is no fertilized egg to nourish, your uterus releases the lining. The blood leaves your body through your vagina. This is your period.

No one can tell you when you will get your first period. You can ask your mother how old she was when she got her first period, but that is no guarantee that you will get yours at the same age. On the next page, one girl tells her story about getting her first period. We also offer some practical suggestions for preparing yourself!

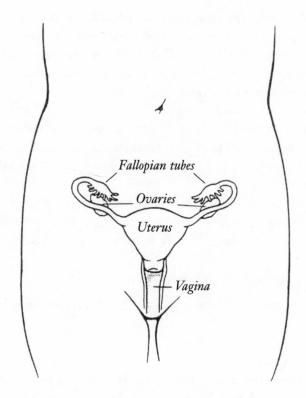

Starting My Period: One Girl's Story*

When I was twelve, my mom talked to me about how I was going to develop, like about my breasts, my pubic area, and my menstruation. She told me that my period could be heavy or light like blood on my underwear, and that there's nothing to be scared of, nothing wrong with me. I was really worried about starting my period, so I was glad that we talked.

My mom also explained to me that she wanted me to know what was going to happen, because her mom never told her about menstruating, so when her period began, she hid her underwear under her bed. She had to go to her big sister for help.

Last year, two weeks after school started, in my eighth hour class my period finally began. I kinda thought I wet my pants, so I asked to use the restroom. When I got to the bathroom and realized it was my period, I just laughed and thought, "Oh my God, it finally came." I was kind of excited when it finally came, but kind of not. And I was scared that maybe it went through my jeans. I was embarrassed that somebody might have seen it. But it wasn't very heavy at all and it just went onto my underwear.

---

*(Diagram and excerpt, pp. 97–98 from *Finding Our Way: The teen girls' survival guide* by Allison Abner and Linda Villarosa. Copyright © 1996 by Allison Abner and Linda Villarosa. Reprinted by permission of HarperCollins Publishers, Inc.)

I went to the nurse's office and got a pad. After school I went to my Girls' Club and told one of the staff members what happened and she understood me perfectly. She got me a starter kit and explained everything in it. Then I called my mom and told her. I wondered whether she wouldn't be ready for me to change, and I also wondered whether I wasn't ready to change into an adolescent from a child. She got all hyper and said, "My little girl's a woman now." I was so embarrassed.

Now that I've had my period for over a year, I definitely feel different; I know I feel older. I thought my periods would be really painful but they're not. The only time it really bothers me is in the summer because I do a lot of swimming and I'm not using tampons yet. So I can't swim sometimes.

Starting my period was no problem, because I knew what was going to happen, what to do, and I could talk to someone about it. My advice to anyone else is to just let whatever happens happen and to talk to friends and family, because it makes a big difference.

When you do start your period here are some tips to consider:

- Talk to your mom, sisters, and friends about what it was like for them to get their periods.
- Know what products you want to use.
- Practice how to use them.
- Keep some pads around the house, and maybe keep one in your locker or purse so you know you can get to them when you need them.
- Know where you can get supplies if you don't have any or run out (like in a nurse's office, bathroom, good friend, or teacher).

Now you know all about periods. Let's keep talking about sex. Here are some more questions from Go Grrrls club members.

I know that you can get pregnant from having sexual intercourse, but I don't really know how it happens. Can you explain it? We can sure try! Sexual intercourse occurs when a man's penis goes inside a woman's vagina. When the penis is inside the vagina during intercourse and the man reaches orgasm, the penis ejaculates semen. Semen contains millions of sperm. Sperm enter the woman's uterus through the opening of the cervix. If sperm reach the woman's fallopian tubes and find an egg that has been released from her ovaries, it is likely that the sperm will enter the egg (unless the couple are using birth control). This is called fertilization.

Now remember that during a menstrual cycle, the uterus lining grows thick so it can nourish the egg if it is fertilized. If an egg meets a sperm in the fallopian tubes and fertilization does take place, the fertilized egg travels down the fallopian tubes to the uterus. It attaches itself to the uterine lining, where it begins the 9-month process of growth into a baby. Because the uterus lining is needed to nourish the egg, a woman who is pregnant won't get her period. This is usually how pregnant women first realize they are pregnant.

I like spending time with my girlfriends more than boys. Does this mean I'm gay? Many people have questions about sexual orientation—whether you are attracted to boys or girls. Remember that there is a broad range of behaviors that are healthy—whether you are attracted to the opposite or the same sex. It is important to realize that you don't have to "decide" whether you like boys or girls. There is a lot of pressure from society to be heterosexual, which means attracted to the opposite sex. The important thing is to relax and go with the flow. Some people change their preference later in life. You may not be sure how you feel now and that's okay. You have time to figure out what seems most natural for you.

? ? Quiz Time • ? ?

Let's see how much you already know about sex. Circle T for true or F for false, and then check out your answers on the following page.

T or F 1. A girl can get pregnant the first time she has intercourse.

T or F 2. A girl cannot get pregnant if she is standing up while having intercourse.

T or F 3. A girl cannot get pregnant if she has intercourse while she's having her period.

T or F 4. Anyone can buy condoms at a drug store.

T or F 5. A girl can get raped by someone she knows.

T or F 6. A condom protects you from most sexually transmitted diseases.

T or F 7. Girls can get a "shot" that will prevent pregnancy for up to 3 months.

T or F 8. A girl does not experience pleasure from sex. Only boys do.

T or F 9. A girl cannot get pregnant if the boy "pulls out" before he "comes" (ejaculates).

T or F 10. AIDS is the fourth leading cause of death among women aged 25 to 44.

Answers

1. True. Many girls think that they cannot get pregnant the first time they have sex, but girls can get pregnant whether it's their first time or not.

2. False. Girls *can* get pregnant whether they are standing, sitting, sideways, or upside down during intercourse.

3. False. It is possible for a girl to get pregnant if she has intercourse while she is having her period. Sometimes the ovaries release a second egg in one month and that egg can be fertilized even if the girl is having her period.

4. True. *Anyone* can buy condoms at the drugstore. You can also get them from vending machines, Planned Parenthood clinics, friends, and sisters or brothers.

5. True. A girl can be raped by someone she knows. Sometimes people call this "date rape."

6. True. A condom does protect you from most sexually transmitted diseases. They must be used all the time and used properly to work. They work better when combined with contraceptive foam.

7. True. There is a shot called "Depo-provera" that will prevent pregnancy for up to 3 months. The shot does not protect against sexually transmitted diseases, though.

8. False. Girls *do* experience sexual pleasure.

9. False. Girls *can* get pregnant even when the boy "pulls out" before he "comes." Small amounts of semen can be ejaculated from the penis before the boy even knows it. Don't believe a boy if he tells you, "I can control that"!

10. True. AIDS is the fourth leading cause of death among women aged 25 to 44. People used to think that AIDS only infected gay men but that is not true. More women are infected all the time.

Did You Know?

Stats on Sex

By age 15, 82% (that's about 8 out of every 10 teenagers) have not had sex.

By age 17, the majority of teenagers have still *not* had sex.

Kids who drink alcohol are more likely to have sex.

At least one American teenager becomes infected with HIV every hour of every day.

More than half of the girls who had sex *before the age of 15* report being forced to have sex.

There are approximately 500,000 babies born to teenagers (15 to 19 years old) every year.

Between 65 and 85 percent of births to teenagers are not planned.

Sixty-two percent of all teenage girls who get pregnant drop out of high school.

AIDS is the leading cause of death in Americans aged 25 to 44, and most of these individuals were infected with HIV when they were in their early twenties.

 Check It Out!

Sexual Harassment

Sexual harassment is unwanted sexual attention—when someone says or does something that makes you feel uncomfortable. Sexual harassment is *not* okay. If you think that you are being harassed, you need to tell a teacher, counselor, or other trusted adult. You have the right not to be harassed.

On the list below, check *all* the things that have happened to you because you were a girl.

☐ Someone whistled at me in a sexual way.

☐ I have felt pressure to engage in sex.

☐ Someone touched or grabbed me in an inappropriate manner.

☐ Someone made a sexual joke in front of me.

☐ Someone snapped my bra.

☐ Someone put me down in a sexual way.

☐ Someone showed me pornographic pictures.

☐ Someone made comments about my body parts.

☐ Someone passed me a note with a sexual comment on it.

☐ Someone asked me questions about my sexual experiences.

Tricky Situation

You and your boyfriend have been going out for a while. From the beginning you touched and kissed a lot. Today is his birthday and you are alone together and feel very close. You begin kissing and touching and feeling really good. Your boyfriend wants to have sex with you, but you decide to tell him that you are not ready. Act this role-play out using verbal and nonverbal refusal skills.

Boyfriend: Why are you stopping? Let's do it.
Girlfriend: This feels good, but let's not have sex now.

Boyfriend: But it isn't my birthday every day, you know.
Girlfriend: Yeah, I know, but I don't think I'm ready to make that decision yet.

Boyfriend: I've never had sex before and I want my first time to be with you. You're special to me.
Girlfriend: No, not now, I'm not ready.

Boyfriend: There's no reason to wait. It will mean so much right now. What's the difference if you do it now or later?
Girlfriend: I want to wait.

Boyfriend: I thought this was what we both wanted.
Girlfriend: We both want to be close, but I don't want to have sex. How about opening your present from me? It's in my backpack.
Boyfriend: Okay.

Questions

How many times did the girl have to repeat her refusal?

What kind of nonverbal refusal skills were used?

What strategy did the girl use in the last paragraph?

Do you think you could use these skills? Why or why not?

Now, come up with some other situations that you think might be risky and role play some of the verbal and nonverbal refusal skills that you just learned.

Having Sex: Why or Why Not

1. In the space below, list some reasons why you think some young people choose to have sex. Include reasons why you might be tempted to have sex.

2. In the space below, list some reasons why it is important to you, personally, to not have sex.

Verbal and Nonverbal Refusal Skills*

Sometimes it's hard to say no—especially to someone you care about—and to stick with it. Here are some ways that you can do it!

Verbal refusal skills

1. Say "no!" or "not now," or "stop!"

2. Repeat the refusal.

3. Suggest an alternative activity.

Nonverbal refusal skills

Body language (such as your tone of voice, gestures, the look on your face, the way you sit or stand) is an important way to communicate with or without talking. Here are some examples of body language that can help you say no:

1. Hands off: Throw your hands up in the air in a "get off of me" gesture.

2. Soldier body: Sit up or stand up stiffly like a soldier at attention and then walk away from the other person if you need to.

3. Firm voice: A strong and businesslike voice.

4. Serious expression: Your best "I mean it" face.

5. Gestures: Hand and arm movements that emphasize your point.

6. Fight back: At times, if everything else fails, you might have to use your strength to push away and protect yourself.

Dear Suzie

Dear Suzie,

I am 15 years old and I have had a boyfriend for the last 6 months and we really love each other. I have been thinking about having sex with him but I'm scared. How does a girl decide whether to have sex?

Scared in Seattle

Dear Scared,

This is a question that many girls your age ask. The answer is complicated! You need to consider a number of factors. Deciding to have sex with another person is a big responsibility. Are you ready for that? Many girls decide to have sex with their boyfriends for reasons that are not very good, like being worried he will break up with you if you don't, or to prove you love him. Sometimes, girls who do become sexually active are surprised to discover that they feel emotionally "let down" afterwards. Remember, having sex does not guarantee a relationship.

You need to be able to handle the feelings and responsibility that come along with deciding to have sex. And on the top of the list is birth control. You need to plan and be prepared if you are going to have sex. If the idea of getting or using birth control scares you, you definitely aren't ready to start having sex! I always recommend using a second type of birth control, like birth control pills or sponges, with latex condoms. Because condoms aren't always 100% effective in preventing pregnancy, you need another form of birth control. But you need latex condoms to help protect yourself from HIV and other sexually transmitted diseases, so it is important to use them no matter what other birth control you are using! Take my advice, if you do decide to have intercourse, use two forms of birth control and always be prepared!

One last thing. Take your time deciding whether it is right for you to become sexually active. It might feel like you are under some pressure to "do it" right now, but remember that there is no need to rush. Respect and protect yourself!

Suzie

Journal Assignment

Who Do I Trust?

In this chapter we talked about sexuality. One thing we learned is the importance of having adults you trust to answer your questions and talk over your concerns.

In the next chapter, we will be talking about what to do when you need help with some *big* problems in your life. One step is to figure out who you can talk to.

Your journal assignment is to write down the names of three adults you really trust. What is it about these people that makes them trustworthy? Could you contact these people if you needed to talk with them about an important issue in your life?

Person #1: _____
I trust this person because:

I could contact this person if I had a problem:

- [ ] Yes
- [ ] No
- [ ] Maybe

Person #2: _____
I trust this person because:

I could contact this person if I had a problem:

- [ ] Yes
- [ ] No
- [ ] Maybe

Person #3: _____
I trust this person because:

I could contact this person if I had a problem:

- [ ] Yes
- [ ] No
- [ ] Maybe

Journal Assignment

Ads or "Bads"?

Remember the information you learned in the Media Messages chapter? (Of course you do!) Sometimes people are influenced by images they see and messages they hear in the media. For this chapter, make a list of the names of alcohol products that you see advertised in magazines or on television. For each of the ads, think about the following questions:

Do the ads make alcohol use look glamorous? Fun? Exciting?

Do the ads show any of the negative effects of using alcohol?

What age group is the ad trying to appeal to?

Chapter 9
When it All Seems Like Too Much

Have you ever been in a situation where it all seemed like too much to deal with? Where a problem you or a friend were experiencing was too big to handle alone? It is important to know when to ask for help, whom to ask, and how to get the help you need. In this section we will learn about some of those situations.

Slumber Party

Caitlin: Let the slumber party begin!

Trinecia: Yeah, but remember no slumbering here!

Sonya: Tonight, lets start with everyone telling something that she never told anyone else.

Amanda: Like, Truth or Dare?

Sonya: That's right, only no dares, just truths. We can each tell a deep dark secret that we've been hiding.

Caitlin: Okay, let's go for it.

Sonya: Who wants to start?

Trinecia: Well, I've never told anyone, so you guys won't tell anyone, right? My mother has a drinking problem. I hate it—she drinks every night and she turns into a totally different person—a really mean person. I'm just so tired of having to face this. And I've been afraid of having you guys over for another slumber party because she's getting worse and I was afraid of what you guys would think if you found out.

Amanda: I'm sorry Trinecia. You know we'd never judge you or your mom for that. And besides, I know what it's like. My father is an alcoholic, too. I don't see him very often, but it's still really hard. I bet I know some of the feelings you have. What helped me is that my family went to family counseling. I was really feeling upset and

I told the school counselor about our problems and he helped me get my family into counseling. Maybe you should talk to someone about it.

Trinecia: But how? I don't know who to talk to.

Amanda: Well, you could tell your mom that you want to see a counselor.

Trinecia: Right! She'd be really mad at me!

Caitlin: Or talk with one of the counselors at our school.

Trinecia: I'm really embarrassed. I don't really feel like talking to anyone . . . but I'm starting to hate my family life.

Caitlin: Trinecia, it can be hard to ask for help. It was for me. About a year ago, my uncle was hanging out at our house while my mom wasn't home and . . . God, I can't believe I'm talking about this.

Sonya: It's okay, Caitlin. We're your friends.

Caitlin: Well, he forced me to do stuff.

Amanda: What? Are you saying he had sex with you?

Caitlin: He didn't rape me, but he forced me to touch him and do some other stuff. It was horrible. I felt angry and sad and I thought it was my fault. He told me my mom would be mad at me if I told her, so I didn't tell her right away. Instead, I started yelling at my mom every day about anything. I just fell apart. But the reason I'm telling you this is that I realized I needed help. I had to talk to someone to get myself back on track. I went to one friend but it just wasn't enough. I needed to talk with someone older who could really help me feel better about myself. I didn't want to tell my mom so I went to a family counseling agency by myself.

Trinecia: But how did you get there?

Caitlin: Well, I called the Help Crisis Line and they found a place that wasn't too far from where the bus drops me off near my house. I had to walk about half a mile to get there.

Amanda: Didn't they tell your mom?

Caitlin: Yeah, you know, they helped me tell her. They can keep a lot of things private, but they have to tell someone if somebody is hurting you, if you say you're gonna hurt yourself, or if you say you're gonna hurt somebody else. The counselor told me that stuff right up front. I was worried that my uncle would get in trouble, but the counselor helped me see that he was already in trouble. And she helped me really believe that it was not my fault that it happened.

Amanda: You are so brave! Wow, since you guys are telling deep secrets, I guess I can tell mine. I also went to get some help once from a school social worker. I've never told anyone this, but I started hanging out with a gang in my neighborhood. And that led me into all sorts of trouble. They had drugs, guns, and some were starting to steal.

Sonya: No way! You Amanda?

Amanda: Yeah, it just sorta happened. I never saw myself as wanting to get into that stuff. But I told the social worker what was happening and she worked with me to get out of that gang.

Trinecia: Did your mom know about it?

Amanda: No, she never found out. I told the social worker that I wanted this secret— "confidential" is what they call it. She told me the same thing as your counselor, Sonya. . . . She could keep anything I said confidential as long as I didn't talk about child abuse or say I was going to hurt someone else or myself. I was afraid she would tell someone but she didn't.

Caitlin: You mean, if you go to talk with someone about a problem no one can find out about it?

Amanda: I know it's scary to tell someone. But make sure they understand that you won't say anything unless they promise you that they will not tell your parents or anyone.

Caitlin: Can you believe that we've been friends this long and never told each other this stuff?

Trinecia: It takes a while to trust people. I guess we really trust each other not to go telling the whole school about everything. Thanks for helping me, you guys. Maybe one of you could show me where the school counselor's office is on Monday?

Sonya: I can take you there after second period.

Trinecia: Thanks. I think I'm gonna sleep really well tonight!

Circle *all* of the possible choices you might make in the situations below.

1. A friend of yours swears you to secrecy and then asks you what she should do about a problem she is having with her family. After talking about it for a while you realize it is a serious problem and that your friend is really scared. What would you do?

A. Tell her you are happy she trusted you but you think she needs to talk with a professional.
B. Tell her you'll be her best friend and help her through this time in her life.
C. Encourage her to tell her mom what is going on and that her mom will know what to do.
D. Let her know that you care, and that she'll be able to get through it.
E. Decide that it is none of your business and do nothing.

2. After starting school this year you begin to get very moody and feel really down on yourself. Unlike last year, you aren't really into talking with your friends and prefer to spend time alone. Your parents have said you seem different and they are concerned. You just feel down on yourself and can't get motivated to do much of anything. What would you do?

A. Get out your journal and start writing all the things that are really good about your life.

B. Call a friend and tell her you need her help because you just feel different and you want to feel like you did last year.

C. Take more time alone where you can try to figure things out by yourself.

D. Call your aunt who really likes you and whom you trust and tell her you are worried about how things are going for you.

E. Stay in your room and just "sit it out."

3. You have been very distracted and not motivated to complete your homework assignments. Two of your teachers inform you that you will be getting a D on your report card. You flip. This is going to be a serious problem with your parents. What would you do?

A. Ask for a family meeting with your parents and explain to them why this has happened and ask for their help.

B. Tell your best friend and see if she has some ideas about what you should do.

C. Call the teen help line and talk with someone there about what to do.

D. Go to the school counselor and see if she can help you.

E. Worry about it and wait until the report card comes in.

4. You have gained a little weight and are becoming concerned about your looks. In a desperate move you and a friend begin to take diet pills. Your friend also showed you how to reduce the amount of food you eat. She has been encouraging you to stick with your weight reduction plan, but lately you haven't been feeling that great and are starting to think this isn't such a good idea. What would you do?

A. Talk with your friend and let her know you are concerned about what you two have been doing to reduce your weight.

B. Tell your friend that you have decided to quit the diet pills and focus of weight reduction because you aren't feeling that well and you don't think it is healthy.

C. Talk to your friend and see if she will go with you to see someone who can talk with both of you about diet pills and weight.

D. Tell your mom what you have been doing but let her know you plan to stop and you'd like her to support you.

E. Forget about it and see what you think next week.

5. Your big sister, who is only 2 years older than you, is starting to go out on her own and date boys. For the last month she has been sneaking out of the house and coming home after being with her boyfriend and doing drugs with him. You told her you were concerned but she just seems to be getting into more trouble. What would you do?

A. Tell her if she doesn't stop you'll tell your parents that she is sneaking out and involved with drugs.

B. Talk her into going to see a school social worker who you know has helped other kids who have gotten into trouble.

C. Go straight to your parents and tell them the truth about your sister's behavior.

D. Go to the school social worker yourself and tell her you are concerned about your sister and see what advice she has.

E. Realize she is your older sister and let her decide what to do.

Answers

If your answers were mostly As, Bs, Cs, and Ds:

You probably made some good choices. This is a tricky quiz. There can be more than one way to handle serious problems, and the action you take depends on the situation. In some of these situations, it would be smart to choose several of the answers. So if you circled all of the letters A to D, you wouldn't be wrong!

If your answers were mostly Es:

You can learn a lot from this chapter. It can be hard to ask for help sometimes, but asking for help is smart. You probably have not recognized the need to ask for help. Sometimes you need to reach out and let other people help solve your problems—especially when they are serious.

Did You Know?

The Facts

The rate of marijuana and cigarette use among 8th-grade girls has risen faster than the rate among boys for the past 5 years.

Girls have higher rates of use of some drugs, like stimulants and inhalants than boys.

One out of every 10 8th-grade girls are current smokers.

Of the girls who report having had early sexual intercourse, the majority (60%) report that they were forced to have sex against their will.

The percentage of teenage girls who get HIV is increasing, and recently, girls account for almost half of all new cases of teens with AIDS.

Girls are almost twice as likely as boys to consider attempting suicide.

In the last 10 years, juvenile violent crime arrests for girls (murder, robbery, and assault) have more than doubled.

One in 10 girls report taking drugs like laxatives or vomiting to lose or control their weight.

Make It Happen

What Can You Do to Help Yourself and Your Friends Avoid These Problems?

Here are some things you can do to avoid these problems. Circle the ones that you think would work best for you and your friends, then make up some of your own to put in the blank spaces.

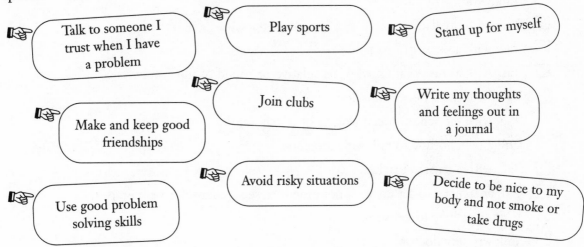

☞ Talk to someone I trust when I have a problem

☞ Play sports

☞ Stand up for myself

☞ Make and keep good friendships

☞ Join clubs

☞ Write my thoughts and feelings out in a journal

☞ Use good problem solving skills

☞ Avoid risky situations

☞ Decide to be nice to my body and not smoke or take drugs

Now add some of your own:

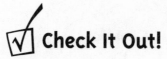 **Check It Out!**

What Can You Do to Get Help?

On the list below, check all the things you could do if you were feeling you needed help.

- ☐ Call a friend to talk.
- ☐ Talk with my mom.
- ☐ Talk with my dad.
- ☐ Talk with a sister or brother.
- ☐ Talk with a trusted adult who is a relative or friend of the family.
- ☐ Talk with the school counselor.
- ☐ Talk with the school social worker or psychologist.
- ☐ Call a teen hotline to talk with someone.
- ☐ Talk with a trusted teacher.
- ☐ Call an agency to set up an appointment to see a counselor or therapist.
- ☐ Visit an agency to get some help.
- ☐ Talk with my doctor.
- ☐ Read some good books about the problem I have.
- ☐ Search the Internet for more information.

Dear Suzie

Dear Suzie,

I'm really having a hard time these days. First, I'm still upset about my parents' divorce. I miss my dad and don't get to see him much. But also, there are some girls at school who have been making fun of me. I feel like I don't have any friends. My mom is busy and coming home very late so she is not around to talk with. So after school I started to invite this older boy home and we have been drinking. He is starting to make some moves on me and I'm feeling scared. I just don't know what to do!

Lonely in Louisiana

Dear Lonely,

You do sound like you are facing some difficult times. The important thing is that you realize things are getting out of control for you. You recognize your scared feelings because they are telling you "I need help."

You sound like you are really down because of the divorce and problems at school. This may lead you to do things you really do not want to do, like getting involved with an older boy and drinking after school. Remember, when you:

- spend a lot of time worrying about a problem,
- or feel like no matter what you do you can't solve the problem,
- or feel scared when you think about it,

you need to find someone to help you. A good place to start is with your parents, your school counselor, a social worker, a local social service agency, a church, or your doctor. Finding the right help can make all the difference in the world! Reaching out to someone doesn't mean that you are weak . . . it means that you are smart. Take the first step today!

Suzie

Paste-Up
Page

Reaching Out to Get Some Help

Get some magazines, scissors, and glue for the paste-up page. Create a collage using words and pictures that you cut out. The theme of the collage is "reaching out to get some help." Think about why this might be hard or easy for you to do and find or draw pictures to represent the theme.

Journal Assignment

My Goals

In this chapter we talked about what to do when it all seems like too much. Working through problems can be challenging, but it's important to remember that we can come through to the other side. We learn along the way. Even when we have problems, it's important to know that all kinds of positive things can be waiting for us in the future.

One way to make positive things happen in the future is to come up with a vision, and then a plan, for what you would like your future to be like. In the next chapter we'll talk about how to do that. Your journal assignment is to write about three goals you would like to achieve as an adult. One goal should be about an adventure, another should be about your career, and a third about school.

My adventure goal is to *(example: climb Mt. Everest or travel to Ireland)*:

My career goal is to *(example: become a veterinarian or own my own store)*:

My education goal is to *(example: win a scholarship to college or go to the local community college)*:

My Personal Yellow Pages

Ask an adult you trust to help you make your own personal yellow pages.

Personal

Someone I trust:_____Phone: _____

Someone I trust:_____Phone: _____

An adult I trust:_____Phone: _____

A neighbor I can call:_____Phone: _____

My doctor:_____Phone: _____

School

School nurse: _____ Phone: _____

Counselor:_____ Phone: _____

A teacher I trust: _____ Room: _____

Alcohol & Drugs

_____ Phone: _____
(Has groups for teenagers who have a drug or alcohol problem)

Alcoholics Anonymous: Phone:_____
(For people who have a drinking problem)

Alateen: Phone: _____
(For children and teens who know someone with a drinking or drug problem)

_____: Phone: _____
(A place for youth to go for alcohol or drug treatment)

Counseling

My school counselor:_____ Phone: _____

_____: Phone: _____
(Offers counseling for one person or whole families)

Help on Call:_____ Phone: _____
(A 24-hour, 7-day-a-week crisis line)

_____: Phone: _____
(Not really for counseling, but a friendly person will keep you company Monday through Friday from 3:00 to 8:00 P.M.)

Violence

_____: Phone: _____
(Assistant principal at your school)

_____: Phone: _____
(Shelter for women and their children who are being harmed by someone)

_____: Phone: _____
(A place for people who have been raped or who have questions about rape)

Sexuality

Remember, try to talk to your parents whenever you can. Talk to an adult you trust. Maybe you have an aunt or uncle whom you feel comfortable talking to. Remember that sometimes other kids your own age don't have all the facts, even if they act like they do.

You can also talk to your school nurse or your own doctor. They can refer you to other sources of information. Ask them about confidentiality. Most doctors and nurses can talk to you about sexuality and keep what you say confidential, but it is important to talk with them about this first.

School nurse: _____ Room: _____ Phone: _____

Doctor: _____ Phone: _____

Planned Parenthood: Phone: _____
(Where people can go for information about sexuality, birth control and sexually transmitted diseases. They also provide counselors to talk to, physical exams, and birth control supplies).

Shelters for Youth

_____: Phone: _____
(For youth who run away)

_____: Phone: _____
(A place to stay for 3 days when it gets to be too much).

Who Can Help?

1. Sally is a 13-year-old girl who lives with her mom. Her parents recently got divorced, and Sally says that she just feels sad now whenever she's at home. She hasn't talked to her old friends in a long time because she feels embarrassed about her family breaking up, and she's afraid that if she talks to them she might start crying. She met a guy at the corner convenience store whom she kind of likes to talk to. He gave her some beer last week, and she thought it was easy to talk to him after that. All week long, she's been sneaking out the back door after her mom goes to bed, so she can meet this guy on the corner. He says he's allowed to stay out all night. Sally is starting to feel like her life is out of control. Who can help her?

In the list below, circle all of the different things that you think Sally is facing.

Depression/sadness about her parents' divorce	Using alcohol	Risky situation being with a guy she doesn't know well	School detention and suspension
Getting arrested	Eating disorders	Not talking to her old friends	Doesn't really have a serious problem

Now look at your yellow pages and list as many resources to help Sally as you possibly can.

2. Ruthie is feeling kind of scared. She has been counting calories in everything she eats and also exercising every day. She used to weigh 150 pounds but now she is down to about 100 pounds. She still thinks that she looks fat. Her friends are telling her that she looks too skinny, but Ruthie doesn't believe it. She is feeling tired and anxious all of the time. Who can help her?

In the list below, circle all of the different things that you think Ruthie is facing.

Depression/sadness about her parents' divorce	Using alcohol	Risky situation being with a guy she doesn't know well	School detention and suspension
Getting arrested	Eating disorders	Not talking to her old friends	Doesn't really have a serious problem

Now look at your yellow pages and list as many resources to help Ruthie as you possibly can.

Chapter 10
Planning for the Future

Have you ever thought about what you might want to do when you get older? Or how to be successful at what you decide to do? Developing some "career sense" now can be helpful as you consider what options are available and what your talents and abilities are. It's fun to think about the subjects you are passionate about. One thing to remember while you begin planning for your future is this: All careers are open to you, even those where few women have gone before.

Slumber Party

Amanda: I love being able to see Cory at school everyday.

Sonya: The guys at school are great but I'm not into school this year at all.

Caitlin: Why not? I thought you were doing great in school.

Sonya: I just can't do the math problems Mr. Griffen gives us. I'm really no good at that stuff.

Trinecia: School work is not where I'm at either.

Caitlin: Hey, I know you can both do well in that class.

Sonya: Caitlin, you're just saying that because you work hard and end up with all As!

Caitlin: No, I have my own doubts but I know I can do better in math when I really try. If you work at it, math isn't that hard to master.

Trinecia: Oh, Caitlin, you're just lucky you've got that math gene. It's easy for you.

Caitlin: Really, it isn't. This year I realized I was giving up too easily—saying to myself, "I can't do math." But once I had a goal . . . to understand math . . . then I came up with a plan. I studied math a little bit every night, I went to the tutoring room after school once a week, and I asked the teacher questions that I had. I found out that I could do it pretty well.

Sonya: So you're saying we aren't doing well because we aren't working hard enough?

Caitlin: Well, maybe you just aren't really planning how to do better. It can be discouraging, though, because sometimes people tell us that because we're girls we can't do math. It's not true, but the more you hear it, the easier it is to believe.

Amanda: Yeah, I've heard people say that before. I actually had a math teacher once who told the whole class that boys were better at math!

Caitlin: Unbelievable! You have to get to the point where you say, "If I really work at this I can probably do fine" instead of "I'm no good at math." You have to really believe that you can be successful if you work at it. If it doesn't go well it might mean that it's just hard and it takes more time to figure out . . . not that you can't do it.

Sonya: She's such a brain head.

Amanda: Me, too! I'm out to rule the world!

Trinecia: Girls rule!

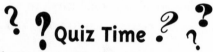

Circle your answers to the following questions:

1. The principal of your school is:
   Male
   Female

2. The mayor of your city is:
   Male
   Female

3. The governor of your state is:
   Male
   Female

4. The Vice President of the United States is:
   Male
   Female

5. The President of the United States is:
   Male
   Female

Answers

Count the number of females you circled. Most girls will have only one or two circles around "female." We have never had a female president or vice president in the United States. Can you believe it?! Other countries have had women presidents and some states have women as governors, but most people who hold important political office are still men.

What does this tell you about women's roles in society today? It tells us that progress is slow and we need to support more women who run for political office.

Are there more women in office today than there were 100 years ago? Absolutely. Things are changing for the better. Maybe in another 100 years there will be about the same number of women and men in powerful leadership roles.

Did You Know?

Who Does the Work?

The following chart lists jobs and the percent of women who work in these careers.

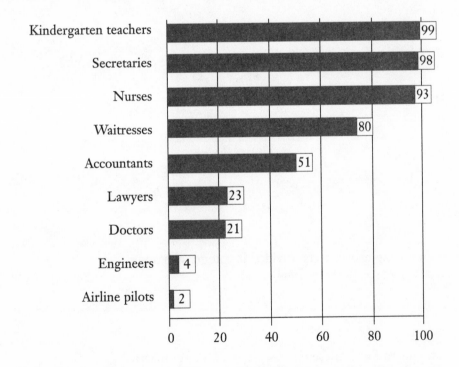

When you look for a job, remember that the possibilities are endless—as endless as you want them to be. In today's world you can be who you want to be. Just do it. But remember, society still has stereotyped ideas about what most women and men do. Scrap it. The woman of today will do whatever she wants to do.

When both a wife and husband have full-time jobs, who does the housework? Check it out.

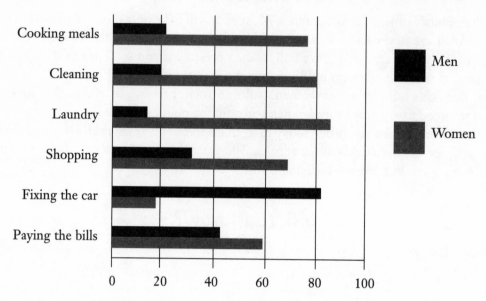

What do you think are possible reasons for the way these chores are split?

What would be fair?

How do you want the chores to be divided if you get married?

How do you want to finish these chores if you don't get married?

Check It Out!

What Would You Like to Do?

Which type of career do you think best fits you? Check the careers you think you might like best.

☐ Focus on **Science**

architect	engineer
biologist	geologist
chemist	surgeon
computer programmer	veterinarian

☐ Focus on **People**

advertising	physical therapist
counselor	public relations director
librarian	psychologist
lobbyist	social worker
manager	teacher
minister	travel agent
nurse	

☐ Focus on **Creativity**

actress	musician
artist	photographer
chef	radio host
director	singer
designer	editor
interior designer	writer

☐ Focus on **Business**

administrator	lawyer
advertiser	manager
banker	sales person
economist	stockbroker

Make It Happen

Write a Letter to Yourself

Do you think our country would be different if a woman were the president of the United States? Why or why not?

Write a letter to yourself, but pretend that you are now 25 years old. How would you describe yourself at age 25? What are you doing? What do you look like? Have you gone to college yet? Are you married or single? What type of job or career do you have? Are you happy with the life choices you made?

Dear younger me,
I am 25 years old now, and . . .

What I Will Be Doing

To achieve big goals, we need to plan smaller steps to help us get there. Complete the following statements to help you plan the steps along the path to achieving your personal goals.

Goal #1: _____

To achieve my goal, one step I will take in the next 5 days is:

_____

To achieve my goal, one step I will take in the next 5 months is:

_____

To achieve my goal, one step I will take in the next 5 years is:

_____

Goal #2: _____

To achieve my goal, one step I will take in the next 5 days is:

_____

To achieve my goal, one step I will take in the next 5 months is:

_____

To achieve my goal, one step I will take in the next 5 years is:

_____

What's Important to Me

There are ten statements printed on this page. Circle the three statements that you would say *you* are *most* concerned about. There are no "right" answers, just circle the statements that are most important to you.

1. I think people need to be more involved in protecting the natural environment: the earth, air, water, etc.

2. I think one of the most important things we could do is to help young kids learn to read, write, and do arithmetic really well.

3. I think racism is one of the biggest problems in the world today, and we need to find ways to help people get along better.

4. I think that our society treats elderly people pretty badly. We need to stop ignoring older folks and help them stay involved in life.

5. I think that people in general have a really bad impression of what teenagers are like today. We need to get the message out that most teenagers are really good people who work hard.

6. I am concerned about the way we treat animals. There are too many dogs and cats that end up in shelters and get put to sleep every year because people aren't responsible pet owners.

7. I think we need to find ways to provide mentors to young kids, to help steer them toward the right path, and to encourage them a lot.

8. I think that people in this country don't exercise their right to vote. We need to make people understand how important it is to vote.

9. I think that we need to pay more attention to people with disabilities. We need to work hard to be sure that public buildings are accessible and that people who are different don't feel left out.

10. I think the world is perfect just the way it is and there is nothing we need to do to make it better.

I chose #_____ , #_____ , and #_____ .

Community Hookups

Now that you've identified some of your interests, it is time to figure out how to take ACTION! Circle any items on the list below that you think you could do to make your community a better place. Then use your goal setting and planning skills to help you do it!

i can start a newsletter or zine about the issue i care about.

I can write a letter to the editor of the newspaper.

I can surf the Internet for sites relating to the issue I care about.

I can ask the school counselors and social studies teachers about volunteer opportunities.

i can join (or start!) a club at my school.

I CAN ASK MY PARENTS TO HOST A POTLUCK MEAL FOR THE NEIGHBORHOOD SO WE CAN ALL MEET.

I can call my local volunteer center to find out if there are places where kids my age can volunteer.

Dear Suzie

Dear Suzie,

I don't know what I want to do in my life. It seems like I'm not that good at anything. What kind of future can I make for myself when I'm feeling this way?

Confused in Cincinnati

Dear Confused,

First, relax a bit. You are young and you have plenty of time to figure things out. Second, you need to know that there are lots of possibilities. Today, women are pursuing all sorts of jobs. It sounds like it's time for you to start to find out about them!

Begin by thinking about your interests and talents or by checking out different careers. Set a goal for yourself to explore your interests or find out about different jobs. Find a book that describes different careers in your school library, interview your friends' parents about their interests or what they do, talk to your friends about their interests, or search the Internet. Finding your place in life doesn't just happen—you've got to make it happen. You're off to a great start because you are smart enough to start thinking about the future now. Go grrrl!

Suzie

Page

Women in the Workforce

Grab some more magazines. (We hope you have some left!) Find some pictures of women in different careers. The pictures of women as models are easy to find, but can you find pictures of women in science and business careers? Create a collage using the pictures you find. For added fun, make up bubble statements explaining why they like what they do. For example:

I like being a lawyer because people seek my advice and trust me.

Journal Assignment

What Did You Learn from Go Grrrls?

Can you believe that you are almost finished with this workbook? (Of course, you can always read it over and add more to it.) Your journal assignment is to circle the topics that meant the most to *you, personally.*

Being a Girl in Today's Society

Media Messages

Positive Body Image

POSITIVE MINDSET

Making and Keeping Friends

Establishing Independence

Understanding Sexuality

When It All Seems Like Too Much

Planning for the Future

Now, go back to chapter 1 and see which topics you circled before you started this book. Are they the same or different from the ones you picked here?

Which was your favorite part?

What was the hardest thing for you to do?

Go Grrrls Graduate

This certificate demonstrates that the individual named below has successfully completed the

Go Grrrls Strength-Building Program

Presented to

_____

for her awesome achievement!

_____
Signature

_____
Date